I0093992

BY-ROADS AND HIDDEN TREASURES

BY-ROADS AND HIDDEN TREASURES MAPPING CULTURAL ASSETS IN REGIONAL AUSTRALIA

EDITED BY
PAUL ASHTON
CHRIS GIBSON AND
ROSS GIBSON

U W
A P
UWA PUBLISHING

First published in 2015 by
UWA Publishing
Crawley, Western Australia 6009
www.uwap.uwa.edu.au

UWAP is an imprint of UWA Publishing
a division of The University of Western Australia

THE UNIVERSITY OF
WESTERN AUSTRALIA

This book is copyright. Apart from any fair dealing for the purpose of private study, research, criticism or review, as permitted under the *Copyright Act 1968*, no part may be reproduced by any process without written permission. Enquiries should be made to the publisher.

Copyright © Paul Ashton, Chris Gibson and Ross Gibson 2014

The moral right of the authors has been asserted.

National Library of Australia
Cataloguing-in-Publication entry:
By-roads and hidden treasures : mapping cultural assets in regional Australia.
Paul Ashton, Chris Gibson, and Ross Gibson, editors.
ISBN: 9781742586243 (paperback)
Includes bibliographical references.
Cultural Asset Mapping for Regional Australia. Cultural geography—Australia.
Cultural awareness—Australia. Cultural intelligence—Australia.
Cultural property—Protection—Australia. Australia—Cultural policy.
Ashton, Paul, 1959– editor. Gibson, Chris, editor. Gibson, Ross, 1956– editor.
363.690994

Cover photograph by Lisa Andersen
Typeset in Bembo by Lasertype
Printed by Lightning Source

CONTENTS

Preface

Ross Gibson

This book is the result of a major research project that was conducted by the editors between 2008 and 2014. The project was called 'Cultural Asset Mapping in Regional Australia' (CAMRA). From start to finish, every term in that title was up for redefinition, while the team, assembled from several universities, local government authorities, cultural agencies, community groups and interested individuals, investigated the many interconnected themes.[1]

The project occurred at a time in national and global history when the most basic precepts in planning, governance and cultural geography were being interrogated. We could not avoid asking, for example, what is a map, a nation, a region and a cultural object or activity nowadays? And what is an asset or configuration of value when governments and their constituents are everywhere struggling to understand what makes good, affordable public service when many old values and systems of wealth-generation seem in doubt? For the world is clearly stumbling through an era when new developments in networked communication, post-industrial manufacture, globalised migration, labour-outsourcing, ecological fragility and extra-national finance have radically changed the agglomeration of 'modern' nations and 'third-world' states that formerly seemed to define planetary politics.

All that was solid seems, again, to be melting into air. Yet down on the ground in homes, workplaces and communities that maintain close ties to each other and to the places that accommodate them, people still enact basic everyday activities so that life can keep on going and growing. Basic everyday *cultural* activities. Activities which often make assets in the form of knowledge and structures of feeling rather than material things. It's something that Indigenous interlocutors in many of the regions studied in the project showed us repeatedly, either explicitly or implicitly: that the greatest asset is usually the knowledge and sentiments generated and maintained by committed community members maintaining relationships and performing cultural rituals, no matter how small and vernacular or grand and ceremonial.

In such a contemporary context where 'the local' contends with 'the global', sometimes in a dance and sometimes in a wrestle, the CAMRA researchers sought to understand what is going on in places off the main roads, outside the metropolises. We wanted insights into what is keeping people strong in their locales. Or if they are there but not strong, what is keeping them going? How much of this persistence is *cultural*? And can we keep track of this strength across particular spaces over time?

We had no obvious map for getting started. But we had a 100-word mission statement. We used it frequently to keep ourselves oriented throughout the vagaries of the project. So maybe the mission really was a map. It went like this:

> At a time when the environmental, social and industrial bases of regional life are changing markedly, planners and arts workers are noting that innovations in cultural consumption and creative practices offer opportunities for the revitalisation of some Australian regions. Fostering collaborations with peak cultural bodies, local councils, creative communities and universities, this

Linkage Project collects and analyses vital data about creativity, development and productivity in regional Australia. The project maps and analyses a carefully inter-related set of regions, thereby generating knowledge plus academic and local training that will be vital to the urgent policy and planning decisions that are looming for regional Australia.

After much discussion, we came up with a seemingly simple research question: how can we best map regional culture in contemporary Australia so that we can assess that culture's value? Inevitably, once we had installed this as the guideline to take us into our selected regions, other questions formed in a queue. For example, to what degree can regional culture be seen as an *asset* compared with the seemingly endemic *debits* of isolation, under-population and stigma imposed from outside on these relatively 'off-road' places? And from *inside* these regions, what are the riches, what are the edges and what counts as culture? Is nature apprehensible as culture when nature is actively contextualised as part of the enriched and sustaining experience available in a region? In other words, can one appreciate and make cultural capital of the weather of a region? The light? The landforms? How much might they be cultural assets? Can regions sometimes be legitimately understood as 'country' in such a way that 'nature' and 'culture' suffuse each other to become something else yet again? Can the city-dominated concepts and vocabularies of planning be usefully transposed to non-urban locales? If not, what instead?

With this book we offer several ways to consider such questions. We provide some answers, true, but we are also pleased to say that more good questions keep on coming and they will lead you further into the fascinating territory of regional-cultural sovereignty. And we are thrilled that as we brought shape to our findings, other authors with special expertise in the field gravitated toward the project too. So, as we assembled their chapters and linked them to the CAMRA material, we saw themes coming into focus and offering new ways into and between several different local cultures distributed across many non-metropolitan zones of Australia.

Therefore this book has a kind of map in its chapter-structure. After this Preface, there are four parts: 'Orientation', 'Definitions', 'Theories' and 'Case Studies'. The 'Orientation' essay offers an overview of some cardinal ideas and emotions that have welled up during the investigation. Think of this essay as a kind of 'establishing shot' at the start of a movie: it shows the terrain ahead and sets the tone. The 'Definitions' section shares some keywords so we can get started, even if we want to start disagreeing almost straight away: for example, how to define 'culture', 'nature', 'region', 'country', 'community', 'development', 'planning', 'asset', 'knowledge', 'map' and 'value'. Then the 'Theories' section takes you through some of the big philosophical and historical issues that soak the CAMRA study: margins versus centres; vernacular activity rising up from the ground contending with government planning pressed down from above; citizenship; place, ritual, memory and displacement; education and intergenerational transfer; parochialism and cosmopolitanism; power and the ascription of value; and oblivion. Finally there is the collection of 'Case Studies' in which we look closely at particular regions, communities and individuals who are using culture in a range of ways – including Indigenous ways – as both 'the object of planning' and 'its principle operative means' (to borrow Greg Young's phrases from the 'Definitions' section).

My advice: delve into the 'Orientation' chapter to see if it helps; go to the 'Definitions'; then jump to whatever you most urgently want, in any order, within the 'Case Studies' and the 'Theories' sections. Read the entire book, eventually, by whatever path meets your needs. The 'Theories' come straight after the 'Definitions' because both sections necessarily speak, in different tones, of concepts and abstractions. And all the time, as you gather the ideas and information, take note of your new questions.

PREFACE

1   The project was funded by the Australian Research Council as part of its Linkage Project grants scheme, which is designed to foster increased collaborations in research and development amongst universities, industry and government agencies. The formal partners were the University of Technology, Sydney, the University of Wollongong, the University of Sydney, the University of New England, the Australia Council for the Arts, Regional Arts NSW, Local Government NSW, and the local government authorities in the Central Darling, Armidale and Uralla, Albury-Wodonga and Wollongong. In addition to these professional collaborators, dozens of informal partners engaged with the project for varying amounts of time for varying reasons and results. This full panoply of partners was essential to the success of the project.

Orientation:
Remote, Intimate, Lovely

Ross Gibson

The project known as Cultural Asset Mapping Project in Regional Australia (CAMRA, 2008–2014) took its researchers travelling through a representative array of regional Australia, an array that was chosen deliberately to comprise a summary schema of all regional Australia. I was lucky enough to be one of the investigators. We selected the particular study-regions knowing that we had to get to the most telling places while staying within our abstemious budgets. So we studied how to run the project from Sydney in such a way that we could see frugally but not meagrely into several 'other' Australias. We wanted the array of study-regions to form a kind of template of regional Australia. We wanted our data and the theses we drew from them to be 'scalable' across the nation even as these theses and data were also pointed and pertinent exactly to the locations that we investigated.

So we made partnerships across a nationally representative range of locales from remote Australia (Central Darling Shire), to 'tree-change' havens and regions living in the aftermath of old-pastoral economies (both encompassed by Armidale-Uralla), to a government-border jurisdiction (Albury-Wodonga) and to seaside enclaves and post-industrial urban outlands (encompassed by the Illawarra, Wollongong and Port Kembla). Much of regional Australia falls into one of these categories and we believe that insights gleaned in our study districts will feel true for people from many other regions that we did not visit. In other words, we have worked to make sure our findings can be taken to heart and mean something to people all over the continent; that the findings 'get them where they live'.

Across the hundreds of unpredictable exchanges that ensued when we investigated the chosen regions, the locals often initiated remarkable runs of thought, imagination and compassion. Time and again strangers shared intimate insights that drew us in close and turned the world around just a little. Daily, we were struck by the importance of creating spaces that are not only physical but also mental and emotional, sometimes to the extent that they are also spiritual, spaces where you can define and make claims for yourself in order to offer yourself more resiliently to the world of everyday experience. Right from the start we sensed how useful it is to mark boundaries, to define locales and regions, to mark them but not entrench them. In the coming chapters you can see that the research gave weight to these first impressions. We grew to understand how you need a solid subjective standpoint – or some specifically located and structured node of everyday experience that can be called your culture – in order to move productively out to the larger world (or network) of others. The more solid your grounding, the more nimble you can be with the possibilities when encountering all the other places and people who make the vast surrounding world. The more robust the local or regional nodes, the more resilient the entire network. (For a good entrée to these largely unmeasurable but nevertheless crucial concerns, see the chapters in this book by Greg Young and Sue Boaden and Paul Ashton.)

As I reflect on the insights offered through the encounters with our selected regions, I keep coming back to a special image in the collection of the State Library of New South Wales. It was drawn by Yakaduna, a rural-regional Aboriginal man, whose colonial name is recorded as Tommy McRae (born ca. 1835, died 1901). He lived on the plains of the upper Murray River at a time when his country was being overrun and reconfigured by agriculture, pastoralism and the European regulations of land-ownership. His picture, called 'Sketch of Squatters. Drawn by Tommy an upper Murray Aboriginal. 1864', is a modest ink configuration, roughly 14 × 10 cm, showing the barest graphical rendition of six silhouetted European figures gathered in a chattery gaggle, gesticulating and standing stiff-legged with their knees locked and their tiny feet trying but clearly failing to grip the colonised ground.

The most striking aspect of the sketch is how Yakaduna has conveyed the paradoxically competitive camaraderie amongst the squatters. Adapting European aesthetics and materials to his own sensibility, he shows not only how flushed with bravado

Figure 1. Sketch by Yakaduna, also known as Tommy McRae, 1864
(Photo courtesy of the State Library of New South Wales).

the squatters are, now that they have entered his country from elsewhere, but also how tottery they are and how poignantly they need each other in their newness to the scene; he shows how much they want to get the jump on each other but also how they dare not isolate themselves in this place that they cannot claim to know well even as they have claimed it administratively. It's a scene sketched by someone who, while still remembering intensive belonging, has been recently wrenched from that intimate state. To my eyes, the picture is a beautifully nuanced study of alienation or stalled belonging. From someone who knows the location intimately, we have a picture of the exact opposite of closeness. It's there in the authorial attitude of Yakaduna and it's there within the frame, in the squiggled figures of the Europeans. For all their bluster and energy, the squatters seem at odds with each other and their environs. They appear unsettled, alienated from the ground they occupy. Untethered. Not grounded. In fact, they look a little bit mad, with their jumpy eagerness to gesticulate and make claims. You can almost hear those frockcoats flapping as the buffeting goes on unabated.

So the picture makes a point. It is polemical. Imaginative too. Gazing on its meagre lines, I can't help but conjure the scene in which this rural Indigenous man was improvising with the new, imported technologies of paper and ink to serve his own purposes, working out how to convey some of the ideas and emotions that were bursting over his cognition and infiltrating his inherited sense of place now that the squatters' powerful new world had come to his ancestral region. The picture is a poetic conundrum in this regard, holding several contradictory propositions and difficult moods in a highly suggestive array. And it stands as a precursor to the great flourishing of imagination that has come, in recent decades, from dozens of rural-Indigenous painting communities.

Every time I look at Yakaduna's sketch I get an overwhelming sense that it was made for us here in the future as much as it was also made in response to the importuning, back then, by some newly arrived settler with a meagre payment or a curt demand.

In other words, the picture was and remains part of an economy that cannot be separated from the grim history of colonialism and the making and marking of regional limits. The picture is part of a history of the modern European metropolis arriving to mark out the divisions between the rural and the civic, the marginal and the central. It is shadowed by large forces of land-seizure and cultural erasure that are implicit but not necessarily obvious in the postcolonial condition of all regions in Australia. (This strong idea is proposed in Emily Potter's chapter in this book.)

What is at stake when you assert your belonging in a rural zone of Australia nowadays? Or when you proclaim your valid knowledge of it? Or your difference from it? When I assay the full range of chapters that follow in this book, I am stuck by how much all the authors are concerned – some tacitly, some emphatically – to understand scales of value that evade the measures of demographics and economics. Scales that need to get measured as feelings, as sustained avidity rather than as monetary investment or enumerated attendance. The chapters all show how keen is the awareness of the value of commitment, relationship, care and intimacy in regions that are not blessed with metropolitan proximity to influence and decision-making. This is particularly evident in Deborah Stevenson's chapter on the forces that shape citizenship, Penny Stannard's on the special qualities of the suburbs and Eddy Harris' distinctively Indigenous account of individual entrepreneurialism serving communal resilience. There's keenness and close care in the memory-work that can hold a community together even when its constituents are dispersed widely across space and time, as demonstrated in Miranda Johnson's chapter on the regional asset-value of archives, which can help communities gel both across generational time and despite spatial dispersal. There's something delicately felt – an urge to care for a place lovingly by monitoring all its present needs and imagining a wide range of future options and an investment in the real value of emotion and imagination – that is shown again and again to be driving cultural workers in 'marginal' places: MCs rapping new bushmen's precepts, verandah tale-tellers and long-distance postmen conveying not only stamped material packages but also sentiments and snippets of community banter and know-how, or museum entrepreneurs taking a punt on the value of puzzlement, adventure and delight in the development of the Museum of Old and New Art in Hobart. All this is touched upon in the chapters by Chris Brennan-Horley, by Chris Gibson and Andrew Warren and Ben Gallan, by Margaret Malone and Lisa Andersen, by Andrew Warren and Rob Evitt, and by Justin O'Connor.

Most of the writing in this book lauds the intimate values that put robustness in a place – values with more than monetary worth or electoral/political influence. The writers investigate how to catch the rich and special sounds and smells, the rhythms and closely felt textures, the particular qualities and rituals that define any 'marginal' place that is managing to survive all the contingencies and exigencies that are so often pushed upon it from outside and far away. The authors show ways to bear witness to the convictions that locals carry within their rural or regional domains. They tally the force and richness of someone's resolve to make a go of it in zones removed from the administrative engines and gears in the cities.

The chapters all show the great value that regional people give to and draw from the *connective* work they do, connective to fellow inhabitants but also to the distinctive characteristics – animal, vegetable, mineral, meteorological – of a place. The extent and exertion of such connective work show how much local people care *about* a place and, by extension, how much they are roused to care *for* it in direct proportion to how much they care about it. In this equation, it is *culture* that usually arises and sustains amidst all this exertion. And this is all connected to how strongly people are compelled to assert (or sometimes perhaps to criticise) and reiterate the particular qualities of their places.

Analysing the customs and patterns made by cultural activities and products can help us understand how strongly culture is used by inhabitants of regions for maintaining the boundaries that differentiate their special home-places from other regions. This analysis also aids the understanding of how diligently inhabitants maintain ritual activities that push long, intergenerational durations of coherence through all the educational transactions that go on in a place. Over extended time, we have seen in the CAMRA project that culture enacted in a region can put verve in a place. This verve has a value that can be described or evoked but that is often beyond measure.

The rhythm of ritual is crucial to this sense of assertive involvement with a particular place because when repetitions are freely given, not just from drudgery, an inhabitant can develop a sense of being *stitched* in to a place. I mean 'stitched' in the sense not only of being attached to the place but also of helping to hold it together, trussing it with meanings and committed affections and patterns of love and obligation that make continuity and connectivity amongst the communities that lodge in a place. Out of such freely given repetitions, something technical and closely felt can emerge: enchantment. With repeated, ritualised acts of singing, storytelling, dancing or making marks or artefacts in response to a particular place at crucial times of their life, creative subjects and stories 'attach' themselves to that place. After a while their identities cannot be imagined as separate from the place. The place gives ordered meaning and intensified feeling to the people, and vice versa. Enchantment is the process of chanting oneself into place, into reality. Enchantment is creative, reiterative and constantly careful. It occurs overtly in ancient, indigenous rituals. But it also occurs in annual agricultural shows and music festivals, in football finals, in ceremonies marking personal and communal anniversaries. It's a process concerned to maintain distinctiveness, to hold firm not only against the decay that time and tiredness always bring but also against malicious incursions from outside, be they governmental neglect, media misrepresentation or the chimerical lure that cities waft at the young.

To find the *courage* (which comes from 'le coeur' – the heart) to work and hold firm like this, you probably need to feel roused in response to the value of a place, to care enough about it and to feel so much closeness that you feel encouraged to take care of the poignant details, again and again, ritually and assertively. It is personal, this moment when you evaluate the worth of so much effort. It is an intimate moment when you make a commitment, and as these moments are repeated, they become heartfelt. And the sequence that follows from such moments − the sequence of care − is loving somehow.

Amidst all the politics, pragmatism and scepticism that are rightly parlayed in these essays, this word can and should be stirred in: love. Finally, no matter how shy we are to deploy this term in the social sciences, these chapters persuade me that this phenomenon − love − looks like the most compelling and all-encompassing keyword to brand the surprisingly intimate domain that has been surveyed in the investigations of regionalism that these chapters proffer.

The love is there in the labour, beyond any rational position description, performed by postal officers in regional Australia, whose years of commitment have made them the main communicative but also affectionate threads that stitch together spatially isolated communities; the love is there in the pride of local surfboard shapers who create bespoke designs, handmade iteration after handmade iteration, that assess a surfer's idiosyncratic body and performance styles and match them to the specific qualities of the breaks that peel off day and night along the local points and reefs of their home coastline; the love is there in the connective work − the travelling, the talking, the deal-making and encouragement − enacted by the local poets, singers, painters, MCs and exhibition and festival curators who are glimpsed in this book constantly moving about their regions, joining people with people, holding ideas, practices and memories firm across the generations, across the absences when people move to the cities or return needing reorientation, across the stints of discouragement that come with being told again and again that you are out on the margins. This is a love invested and emboldened in the bonds maintained between people and place. Felt as a sense of active attachment, this love burgeons in cultural activities, in pulses of commitment, sustained creativity and generosity, enlivening individuals and communities. This love shows how a potent centre can be created in any place where heartfelt enchantment occurs continuously and collectively, rendering margins relative. For a region can be in the heart of the people who sustain it with careful tending – in the heart, not an extremity. And despite the deprivations that might threaten the vivacity of any place in the outlands (defined thus by metropolitans), its cultural activities and assets are always its lifeblood. Culture gives integration to the experience of a place and gives inhabitants something more than subsistence – it gives a centre to existence.

DEFINITIONS

Mainstreaming Culture: Integrating the Cultural Dimension into Local Government

Sue Boaden and Paul Ashton

Since the early 1980s in Australia it seems that claims are made every decade or so that 'a cultural moment' has arrived. This was broadly claimed in 1973 with Gough Whitlam's expanded role for the Australia Council, in 1980 with the UNESCO publication of Jean Battersby's *Cultural Policy in Australia* and in 1994 by Stuart Cunningham who also noted that policymakers were 'embodying a framework for liveability in conditions of economic, social and environmental change'. This was confirmed by the launch of the Federal Government's cultural policy statement *Creative Nation* in October that year. In 2008 eminent cultural economist David Throsby claimed a 'new' cultural moment with the election of the Rudd government and the inclusion of a 'Towards a Creative Australia' stream in the 2020 Summit.

Such 'cultural moments', however, generally refer to cultural policy and activities at the federal level. This chapter, although informed by policy and related federal or national initiatives, focuses specifically on cultural planning, particularly at the local government level. It provides an insight into cultural mapping as a component of planning. And it posits that the cultural planning moment – in which the value of research is acknowledged – may be upon local government right now.

Thus far in Australia a sense of and real commitment to integrated, holistic planning has been either missing or given lip-service. In particular it has been notably absent between cultural and the other planning domains, despite many efforts to provide a shared framework that encourages an integrated planning culture. A stop-start approach to community or strategic planning, particularly at the local level, has exacerbated this problem, and cultural planning has suffered as a result. But now at local, state, national and global levels, issues and opportunities related to culture and broad cultural planning are appearing on agendas. At stake are sustainable development and the quality of local life.

Defining our terms

Grappling with complex terms has been one of the challenges for local government in understanding its role in cultural development. For many, culture implies 'the arts' and creative practice, and this is the case for most local councils. However, culture is clearly more than the arts. And defining culture remains an important aspect of mapping, since what is defined as culture helps shape policy and ultimately informs attitudes and influences what is recognised and what is resourced. So what is culture?

Culture
In September 2012, the Director-General of UNESCO, Irina Bokova, declared that 'culture is what makes us who we are. It gives strength; it is a well-spring of innovation and creativity; and it provides answers to many of the challenges we face today'. She went on to add that 'all cultures are different, but humanity must stand united around human rights and fundamental freedoms'. According to UNESCO's *Universal Declaration of*

Cultural Diversity (2001), culture is also 'the set of distinctive spiritual, material, intellectual and emotional features of a society or social group'. Such a description is essentially anthropological, and it was embraced by cultural planners. This had a number of consequences. Writing in *Media International Australia* in 2002, Tom O'Regan noted that:

> This definition of culture justified both the retention and extension of the high arts system and its limited pluralising to include 'new' forms...But it also immediately gave rise to 'community'-based innovations based on logistics of 'cultural democracy', such as the community cultural development and Aboriginal and Torres Strait Islanders arts frameworks of the Australia Council.

Contradictions emerged between national cultural policies and priorities – such as supporting elite arts – and catering for hugely diverse, local culture which ideally includes but is not limited to traditional arts, popular culture, entertainment, heritage and daily life. On the ground, cultural planners – or their masters – have generally tended to privilege the arts. Arguably, this is perhaps the easiest cultural area to manage. And this period saw governments at all levels backing the arts and placing emphasis on the economic value of the arts. This change in policy in turn has evolved into wider recognition of what has come to be known as the creative industries.

Creative industries
This is a relatively new term embraced by the UK government in 1997 as an economic driver and promoted by Richard Florida in his 2002 book *The Rise of the Creative Class*. He claimed that we are dealing with a 'broad ecosystem which nurtures and supports creativity'. The accepted definition acknowledged most recently in the New South Wales State Government's *Creative Industries Action Plan* in June 2013 is that creative industries are 'those industries which have their origin in individual creativity, skill and talent,

and that have a potential for wealth and job creation through the generation and exploitation of intellectual property'. The industries are generally defined for statistical purposes from the following sub-sectors: advertising; built environment, including architecture, interior design, landscape design and planning; design, including fashion, industrial and graphic design; visual arts; music; performing arts; publishing; screen, including television, film, electronic games and interactive entertainment; and radio. Such lists are, however, controversial and are useful as a guide only. Academics and policymakers have criticised definitional exclusions and the potential to overlook vernacular examples of creativity (see, for example, in this book, the chapter by Gibson, Warren and Gallan). This becomes especially important when undertaking cultural asset mapping at the local level.

Cultural planning

This is an idea that in essence has been around for centuries. Many people closely associate the foundations of cultural planning with the birth of the modern town-planning movement in Britain in the second half of the nineteenth century in response to the rise of industrial cities. Later, people such as Lewis Mumford, in his influential book *The City in History* (1961), and Jane Jacobs, in her germinal work *The Death and Life of Great American Cities* (1961), articulated cultural planning's key principles. These include recognising the human side of planning, with an emphasis on primary human needs, reading the layers of the city and understanding its resources, and emphasising the development of citizens and their participation in cultural life.

Noting that cultural planning 'does not mean the planning of culture', Colin Mercer in various publications including Grogan and Mercer's *The Cultural Planning Handbook* (1995) and *Towards Cultural Citizenship: Tools for Cultural Policy and Development* (2002), described cultural planning as the 'strategic and integrated use of cultural resources in urban and community development'. He also noted that 'cultural planning must be holistic – linking cultural resources to broader agendas for economic development, sustainability and quality of life'.

Cultural planning is also grounded; it is about localities, communities, towns, cities and regions. As Deborah Stevenson wrote in the *International Journal of Cultural Policy* (2004):

> Cultural planning is concerned with how people live in places and communities (as citizens), and with the ways in which they use the arts and other forms of creative endeavour to enhance, consolidate and express these attachments. It is also about the way in which local government plans and manages these processes for a range of political ends, including social control and place management.

Cultural mapping

The late Colin Mercer was a long-term proponent of community cultural assessment as a critical step in the cultural planning process. In *The Cultural Planning Handbook* he described it as a 'cultural resources stocktake'. By 2006 he had progressed his understanding of the term to embrace 'consultation and a rigorous process of detailed research – quantitative and qualitative – into diverse cultural resources and diverse cultural needs'. Cultural mapping is an integral aspect of cultural planning which, as described by Mercer, 'establishes the objective presence of the community *within* the planning process rather than simply as an *object* of planning – It assesses a community's strength and potential within a framework of cultural development'. Cultural mapping is more than lists: 'it establishes an inventory of culture' for that place and in so doing takes a hard look at resources, gaps and needs to inform broad planning for the community. In *Towards Cultural Citizenship,* Mercer characterised the cultural resources that influence culture in a place as 'vectors of connection and translation between culture, identity, lifestyles, values and the economic and social systems in which they take shape'.

Sometimes cultural mapping is regarded as a component of the cultural assessment and research process. In this context it is the process of seeking evidence of how people are experiencing their place and culture. This might include mapping people's perceptions via engaging with particular cultural groups, asking a community to describe the tangible and intangible local cultural assets that are important to them and identifying habits and traditions important to the community. Cultural mapping uses diverse techniques, including participatory research methods that provide the knowledge and evidence base that builds the cultural connections to other mainstream policy and planning agendas. In the twenty-first century new technology-based data collection systems provide sophisticated models for cultural mapping.

Cultural resources

Sometimes known as cultural assets and more recently cultural infrastructure, cultural resources are aspects of local culture, both tangible and intangible, on which people can draw as a foundation for planning a liveable, inclusive and responsive community. One aspect of community cultural resources relates to *places* including topography, facilities and buildings and the aesthetic qualities of these that contribute to community cultural life, community identity and sense of place. These places can include heritage items, significant streetscapes, public art and monuments, public open space, views and lookouts, tourist attractions, sporting, recreation and leisure facilities, and community meeting places such as churches, clubs, cafes and corner stores.

Cultural facilities are also important cultural resources since they are often held in the public domain or have the potential for accommodating cultural programs and activities. Cultural facilities include community centres, halls, theatres, libraries, museums, galleries, heritage buildings and landmark sites including open space, parks and reserves.

Cultural resources are also those aspects of community life that utilise or are presented in these places. They can include cultural businesses, cultural collections, exhibitions, events, networks of voluntary and sociocultural and civic associations. Cultural resources can also include local cultural knowledge, skills and works of art – or intellectual property – which people can use for a community's cultural development such as databases, directories, local historians, artists, Indigenous craft skills, views and vistas and social and cultural services.

Cultural assets can also include those businesses or other services involved in the creative industries including advertising, architecture, arts and antique markets, crafts, design, fashion as well as film, interactive leisure software, music, television and radio, performing arts, publishing and software. These activities are connected through individual skill and creativity and each has the potential for economic development including job creation.

The role of government and global organisations

Cultural planning, including mapping, is often thought of as a local government activity. However, as globalisation and new economic models evolve around the world, driven by technology, creativity, knowledge and content-based strategies, culture is being recognised and positioned as a mainstream planning opportunity. In a broad policy context, then, culture and cultural planning are emerging beyond local government as keys to sustainable growth and to the development of inclusive and resilient communities.

UNESCO has been influential in this area for many years, consistently promoting a strategic focus on cultural policy and planning as a key tool in cultural development. This process began at the 1982 World Conference on Cultural Policy, was further embedded in UNESCO's *Our Creative Diversity* report in 1995, and was placed at the heart of UNESCO's Convention on the Protection and Promotion of the Diversity of Cultural Expressions (2000), which resulted in the *Universal Declaration on Cultural Diversity* (2001). UNESCO's intermittent global *Creative Economy Report* also encapsulates this philosophy, emphasising diverse pathways for cultural and economic development at the local level.

More recently, UNESCO has been joined by the international peak body for local government, the United Cities and Local Governments (UCLG). Its Commission for Culture adopted the Agenda 21 for Culture in 2004. This statement declared that culture is the fourth pillar of sustainable development along with the economy, society and the environment. This laid the groundwork for a formal commitment to cultural development especially at the local government level. UCLG now has over 1,000 cities, local governments and organisations formally linked to its Agenda 21 for Culture declaration. The role of culture in development has been recognised by other organisations operating internationally or regionally. These include the Commonwealth Foundation and also the European Parliament.

In 2010 the *Commonwealth Statement on Culture and Development* was released by the Commonwealth Foundation. It highlighted the importance of the multiple connections between culture and development, and the added value that can be achieved by giving greater consideration to culture in planning and implementing of development programs.

In 2012 the European Parliament's Culture and Education Committee proposed a new Creative Europe framework program, which merged culture and media into a single program that would bring the two separate activities together as a one-stop shop for policy and support activities. The proposed merger of the two programs to meet the goals of the Europe 2020 strategy reflects the realities facing the arts, culture and media sectors. In a globalised and digitised creative economy, culture and media are linked strategically under the broad creative-industry sector umbrella.

The proposed change reflects and acknowledges the research and analysis undertaken by the European Union, but also by Member States, including cultural mapping projects at the national, regional and local levels, and which Colin Mercer and others discuss in *The Cultural Strand of the Creative Europe Programme 2014–2020* (2012). Research indicates that as well as the intrinsic values of culture, the strategic connections delivered by the cultural field are also important to delivering sustainability via economic and social goals.

The evolution of cultural mapping at the local level

'Cultural planning', which embraced and integrated the arts into other aspects of local culture, emerged in Europe in the 1960s and 1970s. These initiatives were regarded as critical to urban regeneration where creativity was linked to place-making and city branding. But the 1986 Chicago Cultural Plan led by Mayor Harold Washington set a standard for cultural planning that was grounded in mapping processes. It was developed over two years via an analysis of the city's cultural needs and resources using qualitative and qualitative mapping techniques. This included consultations with over 2000 citizens.

In Australia in the 1970s and 1980s local government was feeling its way in arts development. Some councils had prepared arts plans and strategies and had employed community arts officers. At the same time a number of local councils were beginning to acknowledge that their core roles were expanding to embrace not only 'roads, rates and rubbish' but also community services. Councils were being asked to act strategically, to gather data and identify needs and to develop plans in partnership with their communities where the council might take on a formal community development function.

These plans and initiatives aligned with pressure from state and federal governments for local government to apply best-practice planning and management techniques to their operations, including strategic planning. This heightened interest in planning linked to councils' new role in environmental planning and to an emerging interest in precinct or local-area planning. Social plans or community plans were also on the radar. And as resources became scarce, groups of councils also turned their attention to the development of regional plans in partnership with state and commonwealth authorities. The era of integrated planning was about to take off and into that mix, by the mid-1990s in Australia, came an awareness of cultural planning and mapping.

As David Grogan and Colin Mercer noted in *The Cultural Planning Handbook* (1995), cultural planning was regarded not merely as arts planning but as a means of establishing synergies between economic development and community development. Cultural plans developed at that time demonstrate general connections between tourism, education, the emerging cultural industries, heritage, the arts, technology and telecommunications, place-making, Indigenous cultures, sport and cultural diversity. However, cultural mapping as a process of cultural planning was in its infancy and mostly reflected the 'make a list' school of cultural mapping with a focus on facility provision, and specifically arts facilities.

Similar developments in cultural planning were happening in other countries including in the United States, Canada and the United Kingdom. By the end of the century, cultural planning was closely aligned with city planning and in particular creative city planning and mapping. Cities had long been recognised as hubs for economic development and books such as Charles Landry's *The Creative City* (2000) and Florida's *The Rise of the Creative Class* were influential through their separate but related research, including mapping research, in alerting governments at all levels to the crucial role that creativity, innovation and, in a global economy, the merging creative industries were playing in the production of social and cultural as well as economic values. The trickle-down effect of the 'creative class' was to prove somewhat illusory. As Joel Kotkin wrote in a 2013 article in *The Daily Beast*, even Florida admitted that 'the benefits of appealing to the creative class accrue largely to its members – and do little to make anyone else any better off'. Their message was that cities – but also towns and communities generally – would ignore such trends at their peril. The key is to use cultural planning and creativity to develop robust arguments that foster support for genuine social and cultural improvements within places.

Sustainability and the fourth pillar

In 2001 the idea of ecological sustainability provided leverage to the idea that culture should be considered as a fourth dimension in the planning process. Until then the contemporary planning mantra focused on economic, social and environmental dimensions. Although culture as a broad concept was generally understood and even embraced in Europe, in Australia the notion of culture was generally taken to mean 'the arts'. Jon Hawkes put forward the concept that culture should be included in the planning process in *The Fourth Pillar of Sustainability* (2001). He also proposed that culture was 'the essential basis of all public planning'. Hawkes criticised the narrow scope of cultural plans: although useful in setting plans for arts and heritage matters, for him they failed to consider and place on the public-planning agenda those matters such as values and principles of community life that are at the heart of community and cultural development. In the evolving climate of conceptual frameworks for better integrated public planning, the notion of cultural sustainability had emerged and local governments around the world began to develop cultural plans within their suite of planning tools and reporting documents.

From community arts to community cultural development and beyond

Why was the journey towards strategic cultural planning and mapping so slow? In Australia, cultural planning is linked to community arts which really only got going with the establishment of a regional arts development fund at the Australia Council in 1974–75. A Community Arts Committee was established to make decisions about community arts grants, and a Community Arts Unit was established as part of the organisational structure to provide administrative support for the Committee and the grants program – including policy drafting, procedures, systems, and communications.

As Ros Bower noted in her discussion paper 'The Community Arts Officer: What Is It All About' in *CAPER 10* (1981), from the beginning, the Community Arts Program was focused on 'the enrichment and revitalisation of the cultural life of the community', and she noted that, 'if the arts are to be securely entrenched in the broader context of a community's culture, we need a wide range of creative activities and ways of enjoying the arts'. Right from the start community arts talked about the 'cultural' context and not just art.

One of the critical early programs of the Committee (and later of the Community Cultural Development Board) was to work with local government through the community arts officer grant program. The program was jointly funded by the Board, and by each participating council or group of councils. Community arts officers were engaged specifically to assist in the development of arts activities within a region or a local government area. This included acting as brokers to encourage artists to permeate and enrich community life.

Up to the early 1980s, Australia's cultural life was described by Bower as impoverished, and there was no tradition of local councils being involved in the arts, although they had a long track record in supporting public libraries. Councils certainly were generally unaware and disinterested or dismissive of people's arts or cultural needs including their needs to actively participate in the arts. However, by 1982 the number of community arts officer positions in local government around Australia had grown from two officers in 1974 to around seventy. And local government was supporting festivals, artists-in-residence programs, community theatre projects and neighbourhood arts centres.

By the late 1980s local government was also beginning to feel its way in the emerging field of cultural development and was encouraged to link cultural development to integrated strategic planning programs. By this time, the Australia Council's support for community arts officers had mainly ceased as it focused on other priorities. But many local councils continued to employ staff with responsibilities for arts/cultural development. In 1990 the New South Wales Community Arts Association published the *Community Arts Manual,* which included a step-by-step guide to assist in the development of a community cultural plan. A core component of plan preparation was the Cultural Map, which was described as 'an excellent way to summarise the key features of your area and to challenge assumptions and clear up misconceptions'. The mapping exercise was designed to feed directly into the next step of the cultural planning process – the specific needs analysis, and at this point cultural mapping was established as a core component of cultural planning.

At the state level, the Victorian State Government launched its first Cultural Policy – Mapping Our Culture – in June 1991. The policy provided little evidence that a comprehensive mapping exercise had been carried out. The early cultural plans produced at that time by local government were generally very light in mapping data, due to limited resources and the complexities of integrated data collection at that time. They were also usually arts focused.

Although the Australia Council disbanded its Community Cultural Development Board in 2004 – establishing an alternative model, the Community Partnerships Program, two years later – its reach into local communities and local government continues through supporting community arts and cultural development (CACD) artists, arts organisations and communities to devise, produce and present projects. All projects are delivered with, by and for communities and result in long-term sustainable outcomes and high quality art. Initiatives in this area are also supported by state government arts and cultural agencies which work strategically with local government often via regional arts boards.

Building on its investment, the Australia Council in 2012 provided funds to explore the feasibility and then subsequently in 2013 the establishment of a new national organisation for the community arts and cultural development sector (CACD). It is anticipated that the new organisation, Creating Australia, will play a leadership and advocacy role aimed at increasing awareness, support and recognition of CACD, including to Australian local government.

Here and now

Support for strategic cultural planning as a foundation for local cultural prioritisation is growing in Australia and also worldwide. (Canadian practice, notably in Toronto, is leading the way.) Commitments vary across Australia, but as 'Cultural Planning Practices in Local Government in Victoria' by Dunphy, Metzke and Tavelli (2013) demonstrates, in 2010–11 investment in arts and cultural development by Victorian councils was $354.8 million, with average local government expenditure per person across the nation at $56.80, up 4 per cent since 2009–10. During 2012 in Victoria, sixty-three of the seventy-nine local government areas employed specialised cultural development staff and forty-six out of seventy-nine local councils had cultural plans, while ten more had plans in development. Almost half of those with plans had prepared an earlier plan, and all but three metropolitan councils in Victoria had cultural plans. Most plans, however, focused mainly on elite arts and sometimes heritage planning and made few connections to the broader cultural responsibilities of councils. This is still the case, with at least two councils – Pittwater in New South Wales and the City of Melbourne – recently publishing narrowly focused arts strategies or arts papers, thus losing strategic opportunities to integrate broader cultural issues and needs into their planning priorities.

According to Dunphy, Metzke and Tavelli several councils without a plan commented that 'it was not due to lack of interest but rather lack of resources'. In line with this, research indicated that whilst community consultation was a key aspect of plan preparation, 'the use of data to inform planning processes was not strongly evident, either to define issues to be addressed or to consider their impact'. This includes the presentation of indicators or targets to measure planning goals and actions. It seems that although cultural mapping and data collection is described in the available tools as a critical step in the preparation of cultural plans, few plans mention data collection and analysis as having informed discussion of issues and subsequent goal- and strategy-setting. This absence presents challenges in relation to measuring the impacts of each plan and it also results in data-free decision-making.

Looking into the future

The National Cultural Policy – *Creative Australia* (March 2013) – noted that the 565 local governments in Australia invest a total of $1 billion each year in arts and cultural activities and this is the largest investment of any level of government. Since the release of the policy, two initiatives have taken place that bode well for the furthering of cultural planning and development at the local government level in Australia.

In April 2013 the first ever National Arts and Cultural Accord was signed by every Australian State and the Commonwealth. It outlines roles and responsibilities of each level of government in relation to the provision of support and services in the arts. Local government's role is recognised as 'engaging the community to participate more in arts and cultural activities'. It also formalises the support councils provide and reinforces the crucial role they play in the community.

In June 2013 the National Local Government Cultural Forum, created in October of the previous year, met for the first time.

The Forum comprises representatives from the eight Australian capital cities and the seven state and territory local government associations along with the Cultural Development Network, the Australian Local Government Association, the Australia Council and the Global Cities Research Institute (based at RMIT University). Included in the Forum's brief is the study of the role of local government in encouraging arts participation. The Forum will set medium- to long-term objectives for local government cultural planning, including the development of informed advice on cultural impacts.

The rise in awareness of the need for robust research and rigorous analysis in making the case for supporting cultural development in local communities and for evaluating the cultural impact of services and programs is a key aspect of this Australian cultural planning 'moment'. It also coincides with a concerted effort by peak international agencies to place culture at the heart of the international development agenda. Recently a number of high-level congresses have been held including a UNESCO meeting at Hangzhou, China, in May 2013, followed by the United Nations General Assembly in June 2013. These gatherings heard well-documented presentations arguing for the integration of culture in the post-2015 global agenda for development. Culture was showcased at these forums as an agent of change and a driver of development. It was noted that culture had been largely forgotten in the United Nations' 2000 Millennium Development Goals. Both UNESCO and UCLG are focused on ensuring that culture is recognised as a fourth pillar of sustainable development, and now, given culture's well documented role as an enabler and driver of sustainability in the global development agenda, a network of high-level global cultural organisations have proposed that it should not be left out of the United Nations' forthcoming post-2015 Sustainable Development Goals. A recent jointly authored 2013 document (IFACCA, Culture 21, IFCCD, Culture Action Europe, October 2013) proposes an explicitly focused cultural goal which states: 'Ensure cultural sustainability for the wellbeing of all'.

Although this case for the inclusion of culture in global planning seems far removed from strategic cultural considerations at the local government level, these deliberations do count. UNESCO and the United Cities and Local Governments are arguing that culture as the fourth pillar of sustainable development can be implemented with two complementary strategies: culture as a driver of sustainable development through policy development; and culture as an enabler of sustainable development through, among other things, the assessment of the impact of the cultural dimension of these public policies based on measurable targets and indicators.

One of the reasons that culture was not included in previous core goals was the absence of, or difficulties in, measuring impact or contribution to development. However, in recent years the measurement of qualitative and quantitative benefits of culture has progressed and, largely due to advances in new technology, there is a growing wealth of data and information that has resulted in accessible and relevant research across numerous disciplines on which to base critical decisions. A significant amount of this solid research data has emerged from cultural mapping projects.

Conclusion

Looking back over the last five decades of cultural development in Australia, we can see that local government services have gradually come to recognise the value of the arts and culture. In 1982 Andrea Hull, then Director of the Community Arts Board, said in *Art Network* that local councils needed to 'go through a period of having their soil tilled' before they could take on an artist or an arts project. Recent research by the Cultural Development Network indicates that, if we can use Victoria as a model, local government has made a significant investment in arts and cultural initiatives over many years.

Yet despite the promotion of best-practice cultural planning and advances in technology-based software applications that promote data collection and mapping, data-based, research-focused planning remains relatively underdeveloped. Attention to the development of research methodologies will be critical to harness culture to sustainable development and the improvement of life at the local level. This will be facilitated by the heightened interest across the world in the development of tools that inform decision-making and demonstrate the impact and value of investing in the arts and culture. At this point therefore, a cultural planning moment *may* be upon us.

Having the Conversation:
Creative Engagement Methods for Inclusivity in Regional Cultural Planning

Margaret Malone and Lisa Andersen

Ivanhoe, in the far north-west of New South Wales, has just one sealed approach road. A local joke runs thus:

> Visitor: What's the best way to get to Broken Hill?
> Local: Are you driving?
> Visitor: Yes.
> Local: That's the best way.

When preparing the material for this chapter, we came across a sentence in Deborah Stevenson's contribution, in which she notes the 'frequent silences' that occur outside of cities, where 'the situation and applicability of cultural planning to places within towns and regions beyond the metropolis have rarely been considered'. There was something in that notion of 'frequent silences' that spoke to what we were discussing, both in terms of what wasn't being achieved – what wasn't working – but also the ways in which new conversations were being conducted, with different 'ways in' for regional and peripheral communities.

Over the last five years, the Cultural Asset Mapping in Regional Australia (CAMRA) project, which involved four universities, four local governments, and peak regional, state and federal arts agencies, has been conducted with the specific aim of countering these 'silences'. A number of research projects were undertaken to gather and analyse information about the density, character and value of cultural industries in rural and regional Australia. Other chapters in this book reflect on some of the specific research projects undertaken, and the innovative methodologies used (see the chapters by Chris Brennan-Horley; and Chris Gibson, Andrew Warren and Ben Gallan).

Borrowing this idea of silence for a while – and how it might be countered – this chapter discusses another of the key outcomes of the CAMRA project, the 2013 publication of *All Culture Is Local: Good Practice in Regional Cultural Mapping and Planning From Local Government*, which we edited. Also known as the 'CAMRA Toolkit', it features seventeen case studies from regional NSW (with one from Victoria) on cultural mapping and cultural planning. Each case study in the Toolkit presents a detailed picture of effective cultural research and planning by local government and/or regional arts agencies and their communities. Examples range from the very simple – such as an online 'what's on guide' in Wingecarribee Shire, which gathered over the years a highly valuable trove of data on local cultural industries – to the resource-intensive, long-term engaged cultural policy planning and implementation efforts by Tamworth Regional Council. Conceived loosely by us as 'recipes', we presented each case study in terms of its 'why, where, who, what and how', with outcomes and resource implications made clear. The Toolkit details useful processes and approaches that regional communities can adapt for their own purposes – some achievable now, others aspirational. While far from comprehensive, the selection – freely available online as a downloadable pdf and via peak agencies in book form – serves as a starting point for further information sharing and the development of good practice.

The Toolkit contains examples of the sorts of discussions that need to be (and are) occurring in regional and rural Australia – pragmatic, considered, innovative and inclusive ones. That is, 'good practice'. This chapter explores what this might mean in practice by looking closely at three specific case studies from across NSW: the Central Darling region of western NSW, Wagga Wagga and Penrith. In all three examples, creative engagement processes were used as the core determining principal in the development of their 'communal narratives' (as expressed by Regional Arts NSW, a CAMRA partner).

What makes cultural planning practice 'good'?

Our obvious, and guiding, question as we identified potential case studies for the Toolkit was 'what is good practice in regional local government cultural mapping and planning?' – which case studies were in, which were out? Our method was a somewhat optimistically peripatetic process of asking around, researching, short-listing, reflecting, delving further, refining and accepting. We were guided by two key partners on the CAMRA project – Regional Arts NSW and Local Government NSW – who were keen to facilitate knowledge-sharing and kickstart a discussion around what is 'good' in rural and regional cultural planning practice. Consultations with planners and cultural development specialists working in regional local government led to the development of four criteria that each case study had to meet: evidence of sustainability and of building from local strengths and assets; confirmation from others in the community that the process had produced outcomes; transferability of the process to other regional settings; and that the process 'fit' with the capacity of regional Australia, where cultural activity is volunteer-driven and creative industries operate on the periphery of markets and up-to-date knowledge and technology. Quite a few case studies were rejected. And while it would be interesting to compile a complementary 'dark side' Toolkit of these discarded ones, it would make for depressing reading. Time and again, combinations of staff turnover, financial cutbacks, volunteer burnout, skills gaps, absence or loss of critical knowledge and unsustainable strategic goals that did not fit the capacity of the local area signalled the end of good plans and activity.

The seventeen case studies that were included are a first step only, but this rich and valuable collection does suggest some important characteristics of good practice. The case studies on local government and cultural planning, for example, included these common approaches:

- enabling volunteer-led actions and structures
- levelling up, and using external experts, ideas and processes when developing a locally-based cultural plan
- facilitating 'access' for the community and local, professional creative industries
- *understanding that 'big things' do not happen quickly in regional Australia and engaging with the community to set long-term goals.*

Similarly, case studies of cultural mapping and data collection repeatedly featured a number of elements to good practice:

- re-use of existing data, such as ABS datasets, to save money
- draw on local government research expertise for data management
- work with a broad understanding of what is local, vernacular creativity
- level up – work collaboratively at regional, state and federal levels to share expertise and save money
- work with the cultural sector to share and use findings, and, finally,
- *employ creative engagement processes – making a conscious effort to engage everyone, not just the 'usual suspects'.*

It is with the final common elements of 'good practice' (in italics on previous page) – creative community engagement processes as a way of addressing the 'frequent silence' from regional Australia – that the rest of this chapter is concerned.

Creative engagement as effective engagement

Where local government had adopted creative – and even 'quirky' – methods for engaging local communities for cultural planning they all admitted that doing so was a challenge, but one that had paid off. Outcomes included reskilled and connected local government staff, enhanced relationships with the community and a commitment to practice that was democratic and respectful of the expertise of the local community.

The Toolkit case studies demonstrate that good practice is embedded in the local and draws on available resources, resulting in a variety of creative engagement methodologies employed. In many of the case studies included there is a certain element of trial and error, and of risk-taking, especially if faced with sceptical council decision-makers, strained communities and limited resources. Randy Stoecker, in *Research Methods for Community Change: A Project-based Approach* (2013), suggests that by initially asking where you want to end up, researchers can then 'work backwards', subsequently determining the necessary methods and research questions. Elsewhere in this book, Chris Gibson, Andrew Warren and Ben Gallan ask 'as researchers, what kinds of research practice are necessary to engage with marginalised social groups and working-class communities as part of a cultural asset mapping approach?' They further note that 'the politics of knowledge production [is] as significant as the knowledge created'.

To explore the question of what makes 'good' cultural planning practice, this chapter turns now to the three case studies, chosen because of their utilisation of creative engagement processes. Such a simple directive! But if the 'situation and applicability of cultural planning', as Deborah Stevenson comments, in regional communities is to be properly considered, then innovative, inclusive and participatory 'ways in' for all members of a community will be required. As one of the team at Penrith City Council observed,

> In terms of cultural planning, if you ask people in our neighbourhoods about arts and creative programs they'll respond: 'Huh?', like what are you talking about? 'I just want to pay my electricity bill'. But by posing...key questions during our creative engagement events – when people are experiencing and enjoying (as they inevitably do) a creative process – it leads people to answer these broader questions differently. The data collected...is more likely to focus on their creative needs.

Asking locals: Engaging residents in NSW's far west to describe their cultural assets

This case study looks at how researchers, led by Lisa Andersen from the University of Technology, Sydney, and Andrew Warren from the University of Wollongong, worked with the Trax Arts, Central Darling Shire Council and West Darling Arts to engage local residents in both articulating what cultural assets were most important to them, and mapping local cultural production. The challenges for the research were that the community was 'over-researched' due to the number of social services evaluations carried out, that there were varying levels of literacy amongst the population and that most information lived in people's heads. (Indeed, fears about loss of information and loss of traditional knowledge proved to be a serious concern for the communities.)

The research team visited Ivanhoe, White Cliffs and Wilcannia with a specially designed, portable video booth with a theatrical appearance, 'The Outhouse', which was set up in prominent locations in each town. Soon nicknamed by many locals 'the

Tardis', The Outhouse contained a chair and a video touch screen that asked the interviewee to respond to prerecorded questions and guided their participation. Responses were recorded by a digital camera built into the wall of the booth and participants could choose to broadcast their responses via an external screen and speaker to the audience outside or keep their answers private and 'confessional'. (For images of The Outhouse – in situ – see The Toolkit and the CAMRA website: http://camra.culturemap.org.au/central-darling/outhouse-research.)

One challenge of this research was to ask the right questions in the right way for the audio recording. Randy Stoecker in his book on community engagement discusses the importance of using both art and technique in research methods. Using survey writing as an example, he notes '[i]t is extremely difficult to write a survey that is just the right length, with just the right tone in the questions, with just enough captivating language to pique the respondents' interest, and with just enough relational qualities to convince them that their response really matters'.

The Central Darling is the largest local government area in NSW. Yet it also has the smallest local government population in NSW and high levels of disadvantage. Residents were not going to respond well to more traditional research methods like filling in surveys. Further, many people in rural Australia, and men in particular, equate the terms 'arts' and 'culture' with 'high' or 'heritage' art forms. Art is commonly understood as painting, opera, ballet, professional theatre and symphony orchestras, and not wood-turning, craft, recipes and patterns, singing in a choir, rom-coms or country and western music. In short, 'art' is 'The Other'.

Thus, when designing the research questions, 'cultural assets' was kept as a deliberately vague term. The questions were left open-ended, designed to elicit the full range of potential place-based asset types: concrete-tangible, intangible, skill, knowledge, design, natural scenery, heritage, climate, uniquely local, introduced… animal, mineral or vegetable. Examples of questions include:

- If you and your family were to leave the Central Darling forever, what do you think you'd miss the most about the place?
- If you got to choose one thing to take with you as a souvenir — something locally made and special to remind you of the Central Darling — tell us what you'd take with and why you would choose it.
- If you could put something, anything, from the Central Darling in a protective time capsule bubble so it would still exist 1,000 years from now, what one thing would you save?
- Think back over the last couple of years and community or arts events, festivals or live performances you've attended in the local area. Tell us about your best time out and why it was such a good time.

More than 100 Outhouse recordings or interviews were recorded over nine days, equating to 5 per cent of the Shire's population and including many people who were illiterate and/or didn't see themselves as 'creative' or connected with the arts, and/or admitted that they had never previously participated in an interview. While in town, The Outhouse got noticed and gathered community members around it, with many discussions taking place around local culture in its vicinity and in local newspaper and radio stories. It was odd, intriguing and fun, but allowed people to choose how they engaged: would you broadcast or keep private? Would you step into the booth and shut the door or be interviewed face-to-face by Lisa or Andrew outside? For the fly-in fly-out researchers, who were not from the region, The Outhouse drew interview participants in high numbers.

The researchers also undertook a number of more in-depth 'map interviews' with local creative practitioners and community leaders. CAMRA used that interview data to develop an online Central Darling Artist Gallery to make local arts practice more visible (see http://camra.culturemap.org.au/central-darling/artist-gallery) and many (otherwise invisible beyond the local region) artists have used their profile in promoting their work. In addition, a series of GPS tracks were created, which mapped less visible tourism assets or local creative practices through 'walking, talking and storytelling'.

What became apparent from the responses was the impact of remoteness and isolation on these communities. It shapes life, both positively and negatively – from the beauty of the clear star-studded night skies to the lack of access to markets hundreds or thousands of kilometres away. In a paper presented at the Royal Geographic Society in 2011, Lisa Andersen and Andrew Warren reflected on how the Outhouse responses exposed the need to find new 'conceptual starting points' for cultural planning and policymaking that would take into account the residents' issues and experiences around mobility, access and isolation. What would a cultural planning policy look like, for example, if, instead of being designed with far-away, densely populated urban cities in mind, it grappled with the lack of sealed roads where 'everything stops' when it rains because district roads turn to mud, low rates of car ownership, the 'black hole' of mobile phone coverage and the lack of capacity to capitalise on the information transport opportunities of the National Broadband Network? Or, conversely, how could it best support a region with cultural assets that include the vernacular, intangible, natural and traditional? Again the Outhouse research suggests that answers might be found in unusual places. Take, for example, Ray Longfellow, postman for Ivanhoe, whose twice-weekly mail run covers 307 km of dirt roads, delivering mail, supplies, communication and just about 'anything to do with property life' to outlying sheep and cattle stations. The first person the researchers met upon arriving in Ivanhoe, Ray is a vital intermediary for a group of artists living on properties in the Central Darling, The Painters of the Plains, delivering canvas, paints and supplies while 'crating and freighting' their finished products to markets 'away' – at a time when Australia Post is cutting services. Ray, who says he is 'not creative', was also a landscape designer (and volunteer builder) of the local park, has served as (and is currently) Mayor of Central Darling Shire, holds the keys to the Ivanhoe Hall where performances are held, helped organise an arts fundraising ball in a salt pan, has encouraged the development of local creative enterprises, and is very concerned about losing the stories of Ivanhoe's past as the older generation passes. With these critical and diverse roles embodied in one person – how would a cultural plan acknowledge and plan for Ray's succession?

'Faces of Ashmont': Place-making, photography and community engagement

This second example was chosen because it demonstrates how a simple, small engagement effort can be quickly effective. In contrast to The Outhouse approach, which was designed as an engaged research project, 'Faces of Ashmont' was conceived as a community arts event and photographic exhibition. Due to its success, however, the organisers subsequently recognised its value as a community engagement tool for planning. Faces of Ashmont was deliberately designed as a low-key activity, taking three weeks to get from conception to implementation. The project involved Eastern Riverina Arts and the Wagga Wagga suburb of Ashmont, a disadvantaged community that, in the words of Scott Howie, Eastern Riverina Arts' Regional Arts Development Officer leading the project, is 'over-researched in terms of social services but under-consulted in local planning decisions'. The project was part of an ongoing place-making initiative lead by Wagga Wagga City Council that also involved police, community leaders, local retailers and the community.

Faces of Ashmont's focus was to create a sense of identity around Ashmont Shopping Mall and to show Ashmont in a positive light. In November 2012, Eastern Riverina Arts took up residency in an empty shop in the mall and over the course of one Saturday, a team of three – Scott, photographer David Maloy and his assistant Jay Taminiau – set up a photographer's studio and took pictures of locals holding a chalkboard featuring their answer to the question: 'What are your hopes and dreams for 2013?' There was an enthusiastic local response and thirty pictures were taken. Eighteen portraits were eventually hung in the shop window over Christmas and the summer holidays. The show created quite a buzz – it was Eastern Riverina Arts' first exhibition with the community and, in Scott's words, 'it felt special and positive'.

Apart from the response from local residents, one reason why Faces of Ashmont is a great example of creative engagement springs from Eastern Riverina Arts' ethically-informed community arts process. Their philosophy is to engage artists with a strong connection and commitment to their communities, and this attitude of connectedness and inclusion was used in inviting the local community to participate in the portrait exhibition. To get informed consent, each participant was asked to sign a release form with a checklist indicating how they would allow their image to be used:

- for the exhibition
- on Eastern Riverina Arts' website and social media
- in annual reports and newsletters
- as publicity for the exhibition and art space

Participants could choose to be identified by their first name, first and last name, or some other identifier. When a number of participants chose to only briefly engage in the consent process, signing the document with a friendly 'whatever' or 'do what you want with it', the project team chose to treat these responses as *not* equating to fully informed consent, and instead registered it as consent for the public exhibition of their image only. The approach was taken that the only consent the team really needed was that which would allow them to make the exhibition work. In addition, when the exhibition finished, participants were given their portrait.

Community reaction to the exhibition and process behind it were overwhelmingly supportive – residents sincerely engaged with the question. For Eastern Riverina Arts, it demonstrated that simple, professionally executed art projects could achieve quick, visible and positive results. In particular, the activity proved an effective way to get input from young people, who are often not consulted or don't participate in consultation. Since the end of the exhibition, the shopfront has continued to be used productively for other creative projects, including the showing of a video made by local at-risk youth. The video will be presented as part of the Fusion13 Festival, but, as Scott Howie notes, it is at the shop in their local mall that friends and family will gather to see their achievements. The creative engagement process empowered local people and gave something tangible back to them.

Penrith City Council's Neighbourhood Renewal Program

In contrast to the previous two case studies, which were one-off events, Penrith City Council's Neighbourhood Renewal Program (NRP) is an example of a long-term, well resourced program where the NRP staff team – place manager Jeni Pollard, community engagement officer Heather Chaffey and cultural development officer Cali Vandyk-Dunlevy – have evolved a cycle of 'engaging-reflecting-innovating' in community consultations to develop local action plans – or, as they describe it, their 'Plasticine Model'. In 2006, Penrith's Neighbourhood Renewal Program was tasked with addressing physical infrastructure and service needs in disadvantaged neighbourhoods. It was to operate across all council divisions, and had dedicated funding. Twelve neighbourhoods were identified, and, every year two Neighbourhood Action Plans were to be completed (the last two in 2014). However, what began as a process to 'fix up facilities' began to increasingly emphasise community engagement and local input into planning. Today, the program is characterised by an engagement and consultation process that focuses on local strengths, uses a range of novel and artistic techniques in the development of the action plans, and builds a partnership between council and the community.

> *'Hi, my name's Heather, I'm from Penrith Council, have you got two minutes to talk to me please?'*

Thus begins the conversation – at corner shops, in churches, neighbourhood centres, schools and skate parks – which develops into a more structured, documented exchange between Council and community. Four questions are asked over and again:

- What do you most like about living in this neighbourhood?
- What do you least like about it?
- What is your favourite place?
- What would improve this neighbourhood for [*insert target group here: seniors, children, Aboriginal people, etc.*]?

One of the first neighbourhoods to be selected for the development of a Neighbourhood Action Plan was Kingswood Park, in north Penrith. Classified as 'relatively disadvantaged' on the Socio-Economic Indexes for Areas (SEIFA), the area has a larger percentage of single-income households and residents living in Housing NSW properties than the Penrith average. During the initial stages of the consultation process, residents repeatedly expressed their desire for a safe, centrally located, well-equipped park. The collaborative designing and planning of the park became the means by which a new relationship was opened up between community and council.

The site for the new park – chosen by residents – was an empty block of land that was adjacent to the local public school. With one lonely swing set it was desolate to the point where it wasn't even being vandalised. Inspired by work done by the Information and Cultural Exchange (ICE) and Proboscis, a UK-based artistic team, among others, the NRP team commissioned professional artist David Capra to work with local residents and particularly children to plan the redevelopment of the site, culminating in a 'creative visioning' exercise held one day after school where a number of arts- and crafts-based activities helped residents in their 'Dreaming up a Park'.

Using plasticine, paddle pops, pipe-cleaners, coloured foil and paper – everything the local $2 shop could offer, really – children and adults produced their own model parks, did drawings, made storybooks of ideas and participated in other fun exercises designed to solicit input from all. The activities were supported by interviews, and video and photography documented the consultation. Over 120 people attended (a good attendance for the area) and many locals expressed how much they valued the effort. When the NRP team heard the school bell go, and the thunder of many feet heading their way, they momentarily wondered what they had let themselves in for. But, as place manager Jeni Pollard explains, 'people in the communities have these amazing stories and do lovely things and it all just comes together – always'.

Variations of this 'Dreaming up a Park' day, as well as other strategies for creative engagement, have now been used in the development of numerous Neighbourhood Action Plans, as detailed in *All Culture is Local*. The process of creatively engaging local residents in planning for neighbourhood renewal, with all its local tweaks and variations, is one that Penrith City Council as a whole has learned to trust. The NRP team recognise and appreciate what they call its 'plasticine' nature – its ability to be continually remoulded around the specific strengths, interests and goals of each community they work with. One strength was the integration, early on, of community cultural development practice as a critical tool for the planning itself, as was letting the engagement strategies for each neighbourhood emerge and solidify only as the relationship between residents and council developed. And it works. Outcomes have included: new social and other infrastructure; enriched decision-making; greater awareness of cultural assets; community ownership of and pride in processes and outcomes; more respectful relationships between council and communities; and enhanced capacity and understanding within and across council. Most importantly, the process changes the conversation between council and community. In terms of the 'Dreaming up a Park' consultation, where previously council's approach might have focused on vandalism prevention, it now opens with: 'This is your place, how would you like it to be?'

Conclusion

A statistic in the Introduction to the CAMRA Toolkit stands on its own to explain why all of the aforementioned is important: 20 per cent of public investment in cultural activity in Australia comes from local government. If cultural policymaking and implementation is to properly serve regional communities – beginning with the understanding that metropolitan cultural policy cannot simply be transferred and made to 'fit' – then good local cultural data is essential. This chapter reflects on a few examples from the Toolkit where creative methods were used to have a conversation about culture and community development with people and sections of communities who are 'frequently silent' in cultural planning. Furthermore, they employed methods that were inclusive, ethical, respectful and participative. Phil Nyden and others, writing in *Gateways: International Journal of Community Research and Engagement*, observe that researchers who do not include 'the knowledge and perspectives of people engaged on a day-to-day basis in local communities, local workplaces and locally-anchored organisations, can blind [themselves] to emerging critical issues. More importantly, [they] can overlook the kernels of solutions already in place'.

By going 'beyond the focus group', creative engagement methodologies offer a 'way in' for all members of a community. The three case studies included here demonstrate how, when people are enjoying and participating in creative engagement methods, they will naturally talk about their creativity and local cultural strengths. And by combining such locally-harvested knowledge with locally-based data, such as Australian Bureau of Statistics (ABS) datasets, a powerful picture can be drawn about a community's strengths, assets and aspirations. Yet, such information and processes need not be viewed as relevant only to that particular community. Again, Phil Nyden and others: '[W]e have also challenged the notion that community-based research is parochial. Community-based research can be a basic building block of regional, national and international research'. The Toolkit was produced partly in response to an expressed need by local government staff and cultural decision-makers to share with and learn from others. Hopefully, the exchanges will not only be horizontal ones, but from the ground up, too.

Acknowledgements

Thanks to all who contributed their stories: Andrew Warren from CAMRA; Scott Howie from Eastern Riverina Arts; and Jeni Pollard, Heather Chaffey and Cali Vandyk-Dunlevy from Penrith City Council.

Mapping Methods:
Using GIS for Regional
and Remote Cultural Planning

Chris Brennan-Horley

Culture and creativity have never been found exclusively in urban domains, yet only recently have researchers begun to examine creative geographies beyond axiomatic creative cities from the global north. As Chris Gibson observes in 'Creative Geographies: Tales from the "Margins"' (2010), attention has slowly begun to turn to the periphery – small cities, regional centres and remote locations – places that don't easily fit the urban creativity script but where nascent and established creative industries can be found. Creative practitioners operating away from dense urban centres must negotiate what Susan Luckman in *Locating Cultural Work* (2012) describes as the various affordances and hurdles that marginality and remoteness present. Detailed mapping of the ways that creative economies function in such places is therefore vital for the development of tailored planning strategies, reducing the reliance on concepts developed from and for urban creativity. Despite being readily deployed in cultural and economic planning circles, the term 'mapping' is usually used figuratively, to describe the categorising of creative businesses and employees and for cursory examination of locational dynamics influencing the creative sector. Taking a more literal or visual approach to 'mapping', this chapter seeks to illustrate some of the possibilities that a combination of ethnography and cartographic mapping can offer cultural planning. Drawing on geographic information systems (GIS) and qualitative methods, in-depth information on geographic networks and the everyday geographies of regional and remote creative practice can be brought to the fore.

Cultural mapping in remote locales: Problems and opportunities

When deployed in the context of regional and remote creative industries, mapping analyses predicated on business or employment statistics are often faced with a paucity of available data. While government data collection efforts such as the census do include locational referents linking employment figures to specific spatial boundaries like Local Government Areas (LGAs), suburbs or postcodes, these measures are known to vastly underestimate the actual involvement of creative workers due to the part-time and semi-professional nature of many creative occupations. Furthermore, low population densities in rural locations can render cartographic mapping useless, especially when disaggregating employment data down either to finer spatial scales or to smaller occupational groupings.

As an alternative to employment figures, qualitative methods are a viable means for understanding how creative work is carried out. By focusing on the workers themselves, ethnographic inquiry can aid in understanding the underlying conditions, opportunities, expectations and precariousness of creative work. In regional and remote locales, revealing how creative practitioners operate day-to-day, and are linked into localised or indeed wider flows of goods, services and ideas, is vital in planning for their future success. By taking qualitative methods a step further and combining interviewing with a mental mapping exercise, space can be brought to the fore – not only in the abilities to spatially analyse results but by placing the interviewee 'in space' through the inclusion of actual physical maps in the interview.

With a lineage going back to the seminal work of Kevin Lynch, *The Image of the City* (1960), and today including research by myself and Chris Gibson among others, mental mapping, or sketch mapping as it is otherwise known, is a powerful means for revealing detailed information about individual perceptions of the spatial environment. Appropriating mental mapping methods for regional cultural planning, a qualitative mental mapping exercise becomes an important way to uncover community cultural and creative industry planning needs where often there is a scarcity of available statistics or secondary measures.

In both examples discussed in this chapter, our qualitative mapping activities centred on an easy-to-deploy, low-tech approach: A3-sized paper maps were introduced into the interview setting alongside a small selection of different coloured pens. Respondents were encouraged to draw upon the maps when answering questions about their place. The paper map had a simple schema of streets and major topographical features, but did not list everything on the map so as not to inadvertently lead respondents (refer to Figure 1). All interviews were recorded for later transcription and analysis alongside each map. Such an approach allows for mappable, empirical data to emerge without precluding the unfolding of detailed narratives during the interview about living as a remote creative practitioner. This method is a relatively simple means to collect both geographic and qualitative data and is easily scaled up to larger cohorts. Furthermore, markings made upon the map can be transferred into a GIS for further analysis either individually or by collation alongside other respondents.

This chapter draws on two case studies where qualitative cultural mapping methods were applied. The first project, Creative Tropical City: Mapping Darwin's Creative Industries, 2007–2009, set out to map and document instances of creative activity in the remote capital of Australia's Northern Territory. The project turned to qualitative mapping methods to document creative activity in the context of a small tropical city, with a diverse population and dominant suburban form. Our paper-based mapping method was beneficial in getting respondents talking and reacting to the everyday spaces of their lives in the city. The mapping interview method and analyses developed during the Creative Tropical City project were then applied to the second case study: Cultural Asset Mapping in Regional Australia (CAMRA), 2009–2013. CAMRA set out to map vernacular cultural assets across several council regions, including the Central Darling Shire region, in New South Wales's far west. A mapping exercise was carried out with Central Darling–based creative workers, with creative industries used as a starting point for discussions around what their community cultural assets might be, where they might be found, and how creative practitioners operate in such an isolated and remote environment.

Analysis techniques

Recent theoretical development in human geography and allied disciplines seeks to understand how cultures, economies and material things are brought into being through relational networks spanning diverse spaces and scales. This topological approach can equally be applied to regional cultural economies, for visualising supply networks or flows of materials, people or concepts between sites. When relational data is imported into a GIS, the system has the ability to display topological linkages between sites as well as the relative strength and direction of connections, illustrating the degree to which places are embedded within wider relational networks.

A mental mapping exercise is one such means for gathering data for later topological analysis with GIS. To illustrate two ways that topology can aid in understanding the geography of regional creative industries I examine supply networks for creative practitioners based in the Central Darling, New South Wales (NSW), and second, through making sense of the complex topology of creative workplaces in Darwin, Northern Territory (NT).

Mapping networks: Revealing supply lines in the Central Darling
Located in the far west of NSW, the Central Darling region covers 50,000 square kilometres of predominantly grazing land, with small pockets of irrigation along the Darling River. The area is sparsely populated with only 1,991 residents, most residing in and around the four towns of Wilcannia, Menindee, White Cliffs and Ivanhoe. Connections over the vast distances between Shire towns and major centres outside the area are predominately by road. During the mapping exercise with local informants from each of the four towns, different coloured pens were provided for drawing upon their Central Darling map their responses to questions about where they worked, where they sourced their supplies, where their markets were located and where the most inspiring parts of the surrounding landscape that influenced their creative practice manifested (refer to Figure 1).

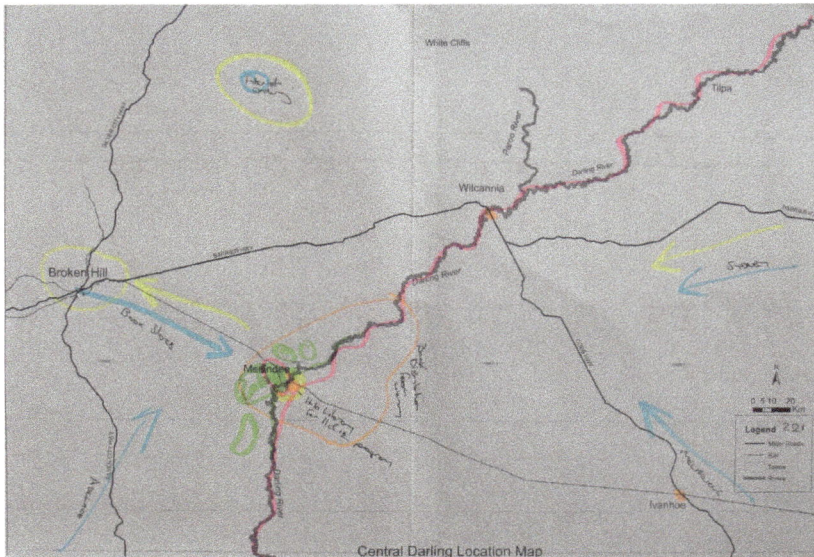

Figure 1. Mental mapping example, Central Darling Shire, NSW.

The term 'supply' covers a range of physical objects and materials that artists and makers indicated in their mapping interviews as necessary inputs into their creative practice. Paints and canvases, camera lenses and batteries, scrap materials from the local tip, wood sourced from nearby forests and opals mined beneath the desert are a few examples of the range of materials that were necessary to sustain the varied creative practitioners who took part in the interviews. These materials go on to become creative end products emblematic of the region and simultaneously are bound up in wider circuits of production and material mobility.

To create the topological maps displayed in Figures 2 and 3, each respondent's map was scanned and turned into a digital file. Respondents' work locations were placed into the GIS database by georeferencing their map (assigning location) and pinpointing worksites. All sites mentioned as being a place where supplies were sought either on or off the map were also added to the spatial database (the map used in interviews only covered the Central Darling Shire and surrounds but many places beyond the map were discussed and often listed along the margins). A one-to-one matrix was generated with a tally of connections between each site. Computing relative connection frequencies becomes possible, for example, between Menindee and White Cliffs or between Menindee and Sydney.

From the thirty-four interviews conducted, twenty-two supply sites were revealed. Figures 2 and 3 provide a cartographic display of the resulting topological network, illustrating supply connections crisscrossing the LGA and beyond. Two types of connections or supply 'flows' were mapped: connections contained within the shire, and connections extending beyond the shire's bounds.

Figure 2 displays the flows of supplies circulating internally within the Central Darling LGA. Lines of connection between locales indicate connections and the arrows along the line indicate where supplies are coming from. Increasing thickness and darkening colour denote greater frequency of connections. In the first frame of Figure 2, only those connections that are occurring internally within a town are shown (for example, a jeweller in White Cliffs obtaining supplies locally). Only a relatively small number of internal connections were evident (seven sites in total), indicating that, generally, cultural practitioners needed to draw on resources further afield than just those of either their local town or LGA.

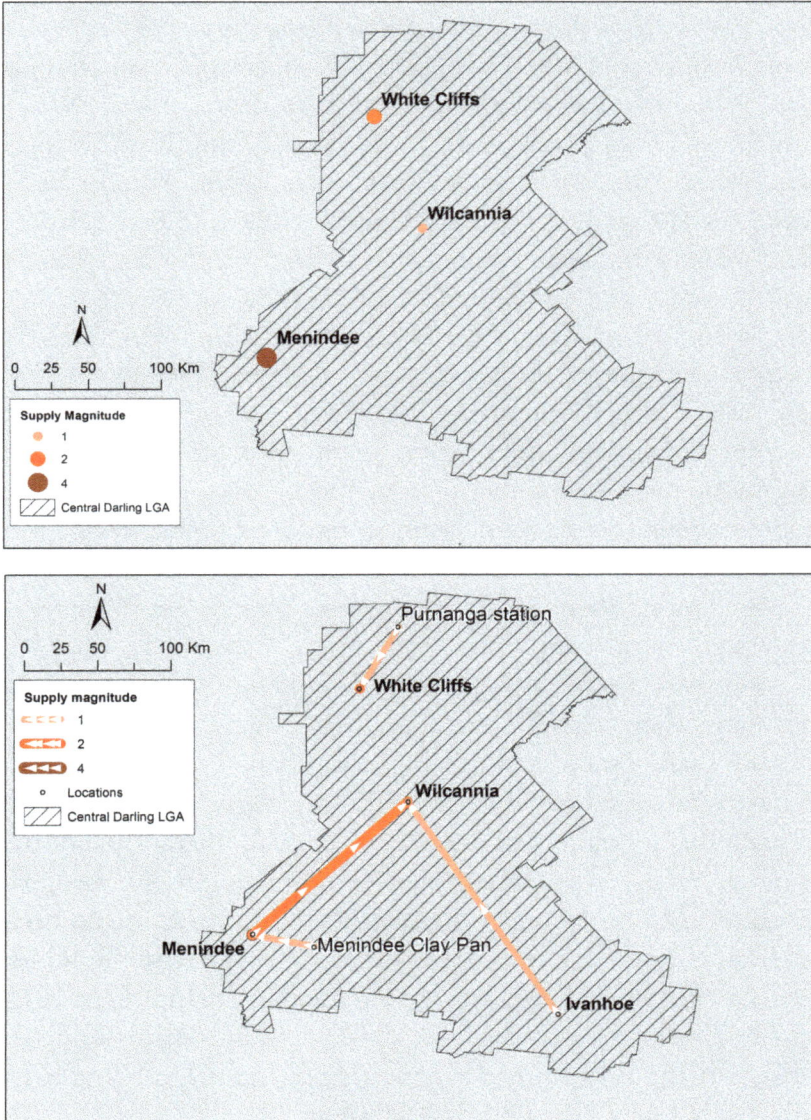

Figure 2. Internal supply flows for Central Darling LGA.

However, simply accessing another Central Darling town to obtain supplies is no simple matter, given the vast distances between locations. The second frame of Figure 2 highlights this quite prominently, with the paucity of supply connections for the region also numbering only in the single digits. The strongest link was two Wilcannia practitioners sourcing their materials from Menindee. Only a single link is evident between Ivanhoe and Wilcannia. No supply links were evident between White Cliffs and towns to the south. It is not only the sheer distances involved in making trips between these towns but, in some instances, the quality of the road network needs to be taken into account. For example, Ivanhoe in the south of the shire has no sealed road linkage to Menindee. A round trip between these two towns equates to around ten hours of drive time but can take even longer due to the variable unsealed road conditions. Dirt and dust take their toll on cars and drivers, and fuel expenses also become burdensome. This leaves many residents heavily reliant on the postal service rather than venturing out on their own to source supplies. Indeed, in Ivanhoe, the local postal service was highlighted by participants as a key cultural asset, providing a vital connection for those living on outlying stations (see Chapter 2, 'Having the Conversation').

Figure 3 displays the spatial arrangement of supply networks emanating beyond the Central Darling LGA. Each town sends out its own somewhat distinct radial network of connections. Explanations for the differing radial patterns are a mix of geographic location, infrastructure (or lack thereof) and the type of creative work taking place in that location. For example, jewellery makers located in White Cliffs maintain connections with other precious gem mining locales such as Lightning Ridge and Coober Pedy. Furthermore, the Central Darling Shire is so vast that certain towns are more closely and in some cases better linked to the comparatively close regional centre of Bourke or other state capitals than other shire towns.

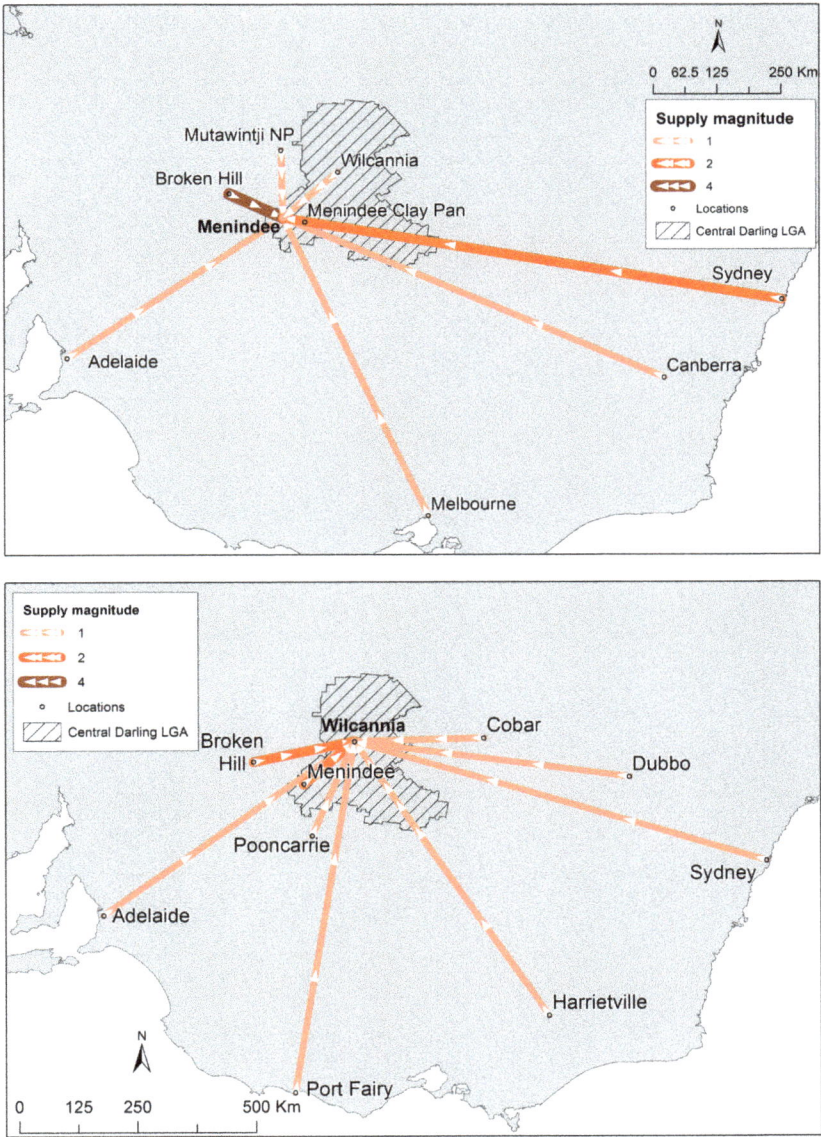

Figure 3. External supply flows, Central Darling Shire.

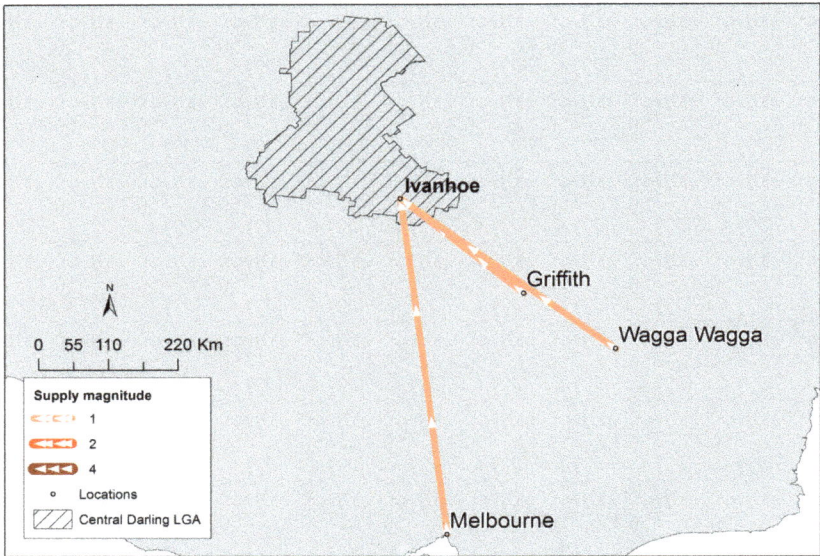

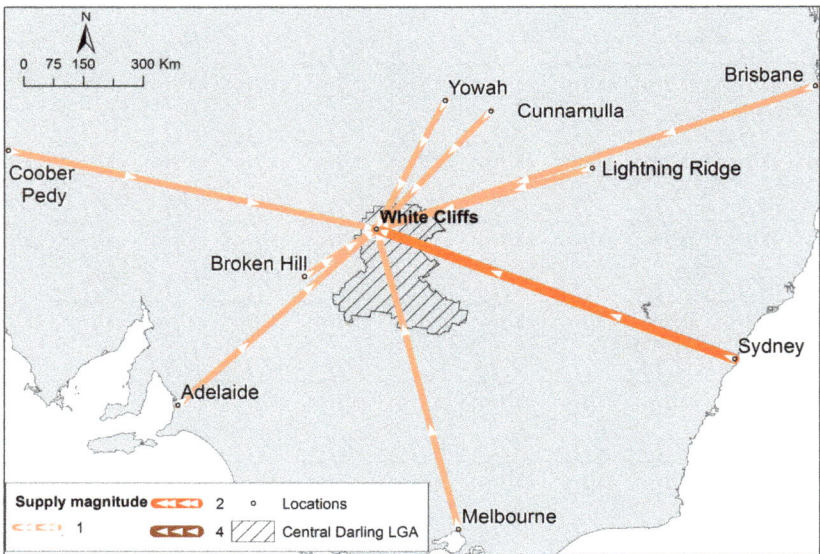

Figure 3 (continued). External supply flows, Central Darling Shire.

These supply network maps reveal a Central Darling creative economy that is heavily reliant on external inputs. This has implications for any regional creative industry strategy directed at the Central Darling, in that the individual needs of each town may benefit from tailored strategies based on the mix of creative practitioners, the peculiarities of their supply chains and how these orientate toward other centres further afield. Topological supply mapping goes some way to informing these decisions but would need supplementing with further topological analysis of product demand (where creative products end up) within and beyond the region.

Mapping networks: Topological mapping within towns
Topological mapping can also be deployed to uncover networks operating at finer spatial scales, such as those between workplaces within a town or city. This second example comes from a mental mapping exercise carried out with creative workers in Darwin, NT. Darwin is a small city with many physical and social characteristics that set it apart from other seemingly 'creative' post-industrial towns from the United Kingdom or North America. Its urban morphology is dominated by a suburban layout, with only a very small downtown area. According to official measures only a small percentage of the city's workforce was employed in creative occupations, yet our research for the Creative Tropical City project found visible evidence of semi-professional and grassroots creative activity, which revealed extensive networks and sites of ephemeral creative activity occurring across the city.

To gain greater insight into where creative activities were happening in Darwin, mental maps were completed during semi-structured interviews with 100 creative practitioners. On average, each interviewee indicated five different sites as workplaces, revealing to us the multiple and varied sites that may comprise a normal working day. For example, a musician might rehearse at home, gig at a variety of venues, teach music lessons at the local high school and record performances in a recording studio. All these sites make up the working life of the musician and deserve to be documented and mapped as part of the city's creative workplace network. Topological mapping provides an excellent means for summarising the multiple connections created by each creative worker as they crisscross the city.

Mapping out the strength of connections emanating between suburbs was chosen as a means to make sense of the data and provide a city-wide summary of the city's workplace topology. Returning to the example of the musician, participants were asked to indicate a main place of work (in this case, the home rehearsal space) and all other sites were listed as secondary work locations. Links can be made between the major worksite and the other secondary sites. Each site sits within a particular suburb and a tally records the instances of either primary or secondary worksites falling within their bounds. A one-to-one matrix for connections between suburbs was then imported into the GIS for subsequent topological mapping.

Figure 4 shows the result of mapping all 377 topological connections for Darwin's creative workforce. A dense network of interdependence between suburbs is revealed, comprising 141 suburb-to-suburb flows of creative workers moving between workplaces. Despite the inner city maintaining 50 internal connections between the 34 workplaces within its bounds, there were numerically more connections emanating between workplaces residing in the suburbs. This reflects a networked interdependence between inner, middle and outer suburbs rather than simply an oppositional binary, pitting the inner city as the premier creative hotspot against suburbia bereft of creativity. Rather, what was revealed were symbiotic relationships emerging across the city, between inner-city locations and suburban gardens, between outer-suburban garage workshops and inner-city galleries. Theories of where creativity is found in the city can be advanced by thinking beyond simplistic proximity-based clustering and by turning instead to narratives that emphasise actual everyday movements, connections and stories. A qualitative mapping approach followed up with topological mapping illustrates that even non-proximate suburbs are drawn together in the cultural life of the city (I have explored this in more detail in 'Multiple Work Sites and City-wide Networks', *Australian Geographer*, 2010).

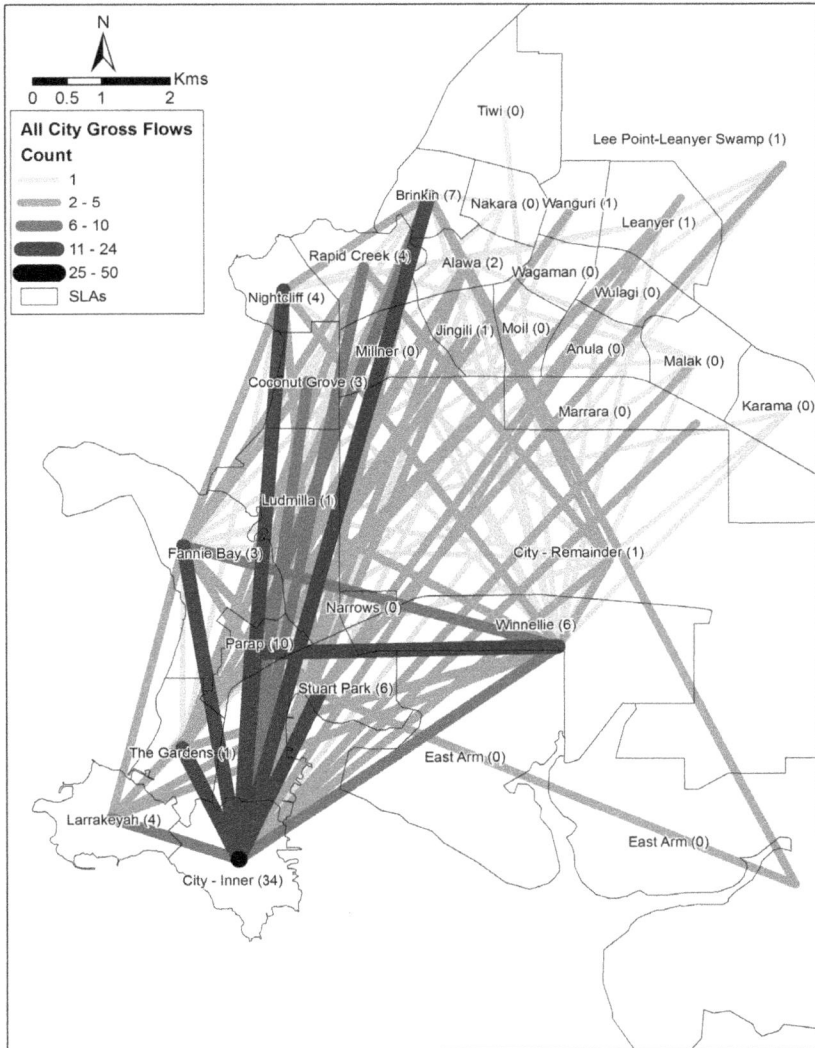

Figure 4. Workplace topology, Darwin.

Surface mapping

Often when questions are asked in mapping interviews about 'where' certain phenomena might exist, respondents choose to denote an area rather than pinpoint a precise location. This data can be imported into a GIS and collated with answers from other respondents, revealing zones of the map where multiple responses were most evident. This section will illustrate the interpretive power of this approach by mapping the most inspiring places for creative practitioners in the Central Darling and Darwin.

Figure 5 displays all thirty-four responses from creative practitioners in the Central Darling to the question 'Where do you find inspiration?' Colours ramp up from light green to dark blue, denoting instances where more respondents agreed that a particular part of the map was an inspirational place. The map is displayed in 3D by exaggerating the dataset about the z-axis. As respondents were asked to mark up a regional map at such a large scale, a fine-grained reading of inspirational sites cannot be discerned from this data. Rather, in this instance, what is mapped is a broadscale regional interpretation of the inspirational landscapes and locales. Definitive peaks were evident, centred on each of the towns where workers resided, reflecting practitioners' place attachment to where they lived and worked. Yet beyond the towns, the wider natural landscape of the Central Darling exerts a discernable effect on creative practice. For example, waterways were important for some practitioners, with the Menindee Lakes showing up distinctly as well as the Darling River, snaking its way in a south-easterly direction between Wilcannia and Menindee. There was also an indication from some respondents of the affective qualities of mobility. Driving through the desert and negotiating a variable road infrastructure can be seen in the main roads rising from the map, highlighting the sparse arterial network connecting each of the towns. The affective qualities of outback mobility, including experiencing the wide open landscapes and the desert light while driving at different times of the day, exert an inspiring influence on creative practice.

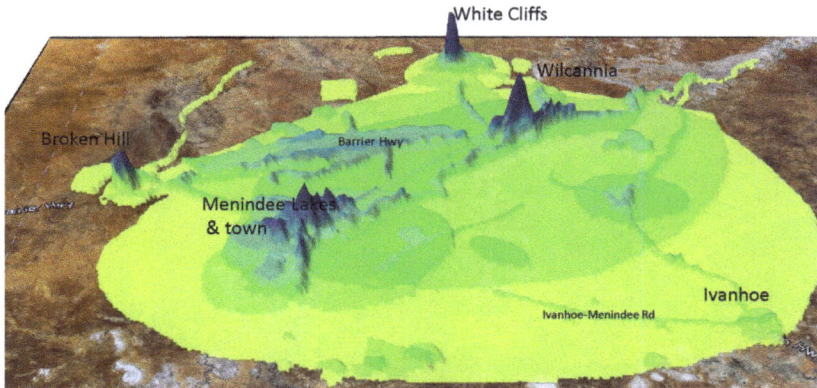

Figure 5. Spaces of creative inspiration, Central Darling Shire.

Turning now to a similar line of questioning conducted with Darwin's creative practitioners, Figure 6 maps the spatial distribution of Darwin's most inspirational places. Evident in the resulting map was a strong correlation between elements of the natural environment – the coastlines, parks and gardens – and an inspiring quality that influenced creativity. In particular there was a propensity amongst respondents to note down shorelines, especially the picturesque headlands and beaches of Fannie Bay and Nightcliff.

The outdoors were viewed as places where designers, visual artists and photographers could source inspiration and, in some instances, insert the locale directly into an artwork, a magazine article or a photographic piece. Others whose creative practice centred on performance spoke more of the indirect and affective qualities of Darwin's parks and gardens. These were described repeatedly as a place to come and unwind and reflect upon their creative practice. A musician put it to us this way:

> Yeah, I find being outdoors [inspiring] because, things come to you a bit more, you can relax more, I find I relax more when I'm outdoors and when I'm near water…I can start the creative process by sitting down with my notepad and writing stuff out.

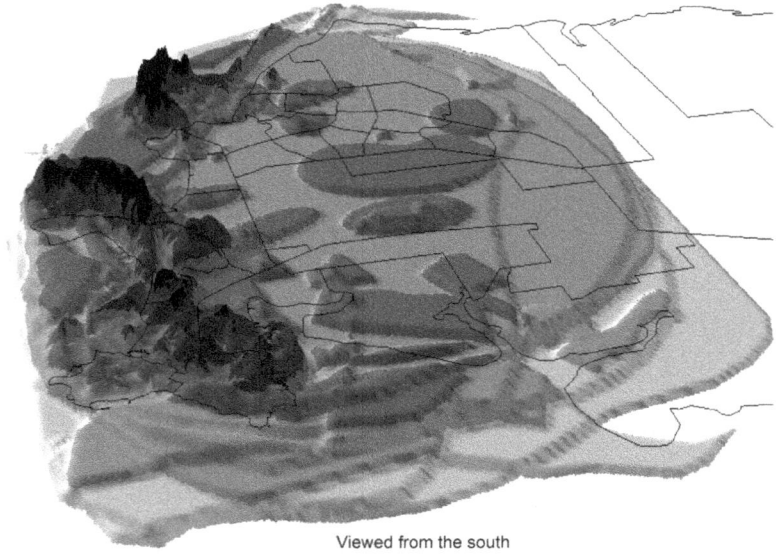

Viewed from the south

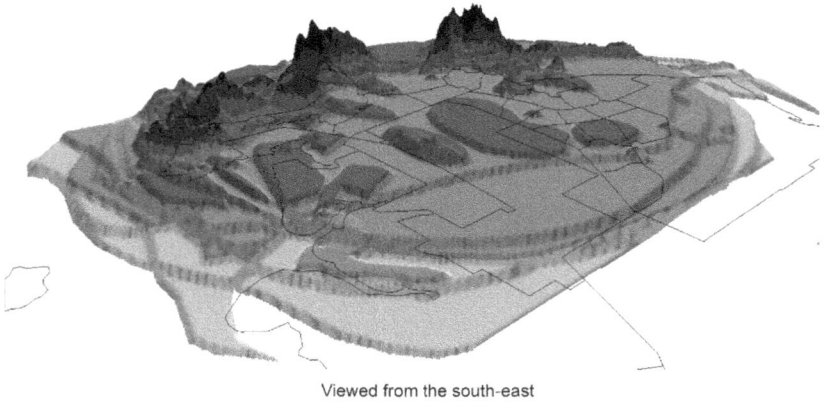

Viewed from the south-east

Figure 6. Spaces of creative inspiration, Darwin.

In a different sense then to more strict definitions of what are creative workplaces and the tasks that fall under the category of 'work', Darwin's natural environment was both a primary and secondary source of inspiration, necessary to the functioning of the wider creative economy. Future spatial planning decisions should recognise and value Darwin's open spaces, especially as the foreshores come under increasing pressure from high-rise construction. Future developments need to be sympathetic not only to physical changes such as views and access, but also to the impacts that increasing use of these areas may exert on the overall feel of these vital open spaces. This point is shared by Susan Luckman in *Locating Cultural Work* (2012). In contrast then to the dense networks and clusters evident in urban creative milieu, access to and the sense of space provided by the natural environment is perhaps the unique competitive advantage that rural, regional and remote places can provide to regional creative economies.

Conclusion

Combining ethnographic methods such as interviewing with the spatial analysis possibilities of GIS provides creative industry researchers with a productive means for generating new and valuable insights about how creative economies function beyond the inner city and beyond the realm of quantitative employment statistics. Methods sympathetic to the everyday experiences of creative workers were needed to uncover how creative economies operate in places without obvious creative clusters or hubs. In the Darwin examples, qualitative mappings of inspiration and work went beyond the usual creative city script that fetes downtown zones as the hotbeds of creative production and consumption. Darwin's urban form precludes that kind of interaction which might give rise to creative clusters full of knowledge-workers living and working in close proximity. But instead of assuming that Darwin is 'uncreative' for not displaying those particular attributes, the results from the mapping exercise present a much more nuanced picture of creative life in a small, remote city.

Creative geographies generated through mental mapping are often messy, and may not neatly intersect. For example, Darwin's geography of inspiration was vastly different to that of its creative workplace topology. In the Central Darling, the patterning of supply lines, while useful for understanding how the region's creative economy ties into wider flows and consumption practices, say little about the everyday affective relations between creative practitioners and their landscape. However, qualitative mapping and GIS provide a way to triangulate between different results and data streams, inviting us to broaden our conceptions about what can be mapped about rural, regional and remote creative economies. Physical arts and cultural infrastructure like halls, galleries or workshops are important but mapping other, more intangible, embodied qualities of place are vital in understanding what is unique in rural, regional and remote creativity.

THEORIES

Postcolonial Atmospheres: Recalling Our Shadow Places

Emily Potter

There's a lake in the middle of Federation Square, in Melbourne's CBD – a lake made of Kimberley sandstone. It swirls and flows although its material form is fixed, and it rises uphill, spreading out over the square's undulating surface. Most visitors don't realise the lake's presence even as they walk through its pink stone waters. Nor do they realise that this lake doesn't belong to the banks of the Yarra, or even to Melbourne. *This* lake is Lake Tyrrell, while its salt-watery form is located many hundreds of kilometres away in the Mallee country of north-western Victoria.

In a country that so often suffers a lack of water, a lake made of stone might seem a cruel kind of joke, or at best a mimetic take on the state of many lakes in south-eastern Australia. As salt lakes such as Lake Tyrrell ebb or dry, the retreating waters leave a sparkling bed of pink salt behind. But there are other ways in which to think about the presence of this lake in the heart of Melbourne. One of these ways concerns the ongoing challenge of belonging in a country damaged by years of colonial practices, and another relates to the possibilities of generating postcolonial ways of thinking about and being in place.

The relevance of these concerns to the question of cultural assets lies in the calculative mode normally applied to the designation of 'asset' – something of value that is transactable; something, essentially, that people want. The 'ruins of colonisation', as Chris Healy phrased it (1997), are generally not this. Damaged environments, like uneasy histories of violence and dispossession, are not familiar touchstones of community wellbeing. Rather, they tend to be excised, both in physical and imaginary terms, and placed beyond the periphery of those things that we designate as valued.

Yet this, like all practices, has its limits. On the other side of value is a shadow reality that continues on, despite its excision from view and cultural significance. What might happen if we turned towards these shadows, if we admitted them into our calculations of a good life, and a good life in place? Lake Tyrrell at Federation Square will be our guide here as we take a tour through some of the shadow realities that come into relief if we interrogate our conventions of value, and bring in from the outside the multidimensions of place. As we do so, this chapter will argue, we may find the emergence of a postcolonial atmosphere within which new conditions of inhabitation unfold.

Lake Tyrrell in the Mallee

In March 2009, Peter Ker reported in the *Age*, authorities came close to declaring that Australia's first climate-change refugees were amongst the communities of the Victorian Mallee country. This semi-arid region in the south-east of Australia has long been associated with drought and hardship. When the surveyors arrived in the mid-nineteenth century, their impression was bleak. Geoff Durham, in *Wyperfeld: Australia's First Mallee National Park* (2001), records the opinion of A. J. Skene: 'this district presents a scrubby, sandy waste, almost entirely destitute of fresh water and grass, and therefore unavailable to human industry'.

Yet it wasn't long before the clearing of the Mallee for irrigated agriculture began in earnest, and this continued well into the twentieth century. While rainfall in this area is innately variable, the severity and length of drought periods, linked to widespread deforestation, has intensified. Soil erosion, rising salinity and dust storms are pervasive. The region has been notably warming since 1950, at a rate of 0.1 per cent degree Celsius per decade. It is widely accepted that this is the result of human-induced climate change as, for example, observed by the Victorian Government in its 2008 publication 'Climate Change in the Mallee'. With its economic base dependent upon these increasingly precarious environmental conditions, Mallee communities are under a great deal of social and economic stress. As the writer Chloe Hooper described in 'Take Me to the River' (2007), an article written after visiting the Mallee in 2007, 'the ground looks blasted, like the site of a battle – which it once was. It was a great battle to clear these lands, one that took heroic labour'. Now the battle has turned. As a farmer interviewed by Hooper explained, 'the last few years our rainfall has slowly diminished, but the last few have been like murder, like being shot at. Only nature can win'.

Around this time, between 2006 and 2008, I undertook several trips with my then research collaborator Paul Carter to parts of the Mallee country and the adjacent Wimmera. We were following the biographic trail of the Mallee lyric poet John Shaw Neilson, who lived much of his working life in the region, initially farming selections and then, when these endeavours failed, taking on labouring work such as land clearing and fencing. Neilson was critical of the impacts of the physical work he was engaged in and could see in the regular dust storms already visiting the Mallee that the environmental consequences of non-Indigenous settlement were significant.

In following Neilson, we visited many of the Mallee's significant towns, most of which still welcome visitors with gracious nineteenth-century-designed main streets. Upon arrival, these places don't necessarily make obvious the troubles that environmental change has brought. This begins to become apparent in small ways: a shop window sign in Wedderburn that invites local men to a 'support group'; a cascade of pamphlets in the Sea Lake local council offices offering advice and services on matters such as income management, re-skilling and suicide prevention. In the promisingly named Hopetoun, a boat ramp runs down to the dry lake bed of Lake Lascelles. The picnic tables that surround this now empty lake sit baking in the sun.

Neilson was born in the Coonawarra region of South Australia in 1872, a place now golden-coloured with infrequent rain. One hundred years ago, however, there were wetlands here, pocked with swamps and teaming with birdlife. The land still remembers this history, and inclines down to the low swampland, while trees still stand clumped together in their wetland poses. Even water grasses grow on the shores of the ghostly swamps. But the water has gone, and with it the birds and the entire water and soil ecology that the swamps were part of. Water is palpably absent across this region; it shadows the drying realities of an environment that has been transformed since Neilson once knew it.

Neilson's Mallee labours took him to another watery environment: Lake Tyrrell near the small town of Sea Lake. Once part of an inland sea, as its adjacent township suggests, the innately salty waters of Lake Tyrrell have become a barometer of wider environmental conditions in the region. While in Neilson's day this lake held water and its creek system flowed, it is now substantially dry. As its surrounding land has been cleared, salt levels have risen, destroying the riparian vegetation that hugs its shores. Anecdotally, we heard that in summer the heat coming off the dry surface of the lake is so fierce that clouds will part as they roll overhead, causing the lake – and surrounding farmland – to miss out on rain.

When Paul and I visited the lake, I was struck by the sound of silence. It pressed close on my ears. In the sunlight, the salt crust of the lake glittered like a field of stars. At first the salt crust didn't – wouldn't – register our presence. We seemingly skated across it. Eventually it cracked, splintering through with soft wet sand. The *Collected Verse of John Shaw Neilson* (2012) contains some of the many poems Neilson wrote while working near the lake. One is called 'The Dive', which evokes the histories located within the seemingly flat surface of the lake. 'I who go diving/ Talk with dead men', Neilson writes, 'At the sunrise I come up/ To the fields again'. Standing on the lake bed, we couldn't help but be struck by the discordance of this title. Who, Paul asked out loud, would think of diving here? The idea of diving into this lake now, of course, could only ever be metaphoric – much like taking a boat trip on the dry lake bed of Lake Lascelles. But even in Neilson's day, the possibility was striking for the contrast it suggests with the culture of land practice dominant at the time. Neilson himself was uprooting trees and laying fences. The land was being transformed into a two-dimensional plane, a series of agricultural squares, mapped and ploughed, with its surface sewn.

Neilson's dive evokes a forgotten third dimension to this environment: not just a fall into water but a movement through air – the density, that is, of a living, breathing place, redolent with histories. There is a certain thickness to the air of the Mallee, even on a day of clear blue skies. Perhaps it was the pressing silence and the refraction of light. But it felt like air with depth, air out of which things can materialise – different forms, different rhythms. The air makes a new zone for relations, a multidimensional atmosphere. It gives shape to a place as it becomes. This is the problem with our colonial history of place-making. As it closes out this dimension it shuts down possibilities for dynamic exchanges across time and space. And yet, as Neilson knew, even as he participated in the environmental transformation of the Mallee, this other dimension is never entirely erased. The multidimensionality of place, even the most damaged of places, is always there to be recalled.

Shadow places

This third dimension is a 'shadow place' in the sense developed by Val Plumwood, in her 2008 critique of contemporary environmental theory, 'Shadow Places and the Politics of Dwelling'. In particular, Plumwood takes issue with the singularisation of place in accounts of what it means to belong and to be in one's place. What she means by this is that dominant understandings of being meaningfully in place, in mutually sustaining ways, rely on uncomplicated and romantic views of what place is – generally, a bordered locale with its own internal logic that bears no relation to a broader world outside (evident, for instance, in self-sufficiency discourse). 'One's place', in these terms, is where meaning is made. In this singular version of place, she argues, a 'suppressed alternative' to how we might imagine ourselves lurks. This alternative is to recognise what Plumwood calls the 'multiple disregarded places' that 'provide our material and ecological support'.

Plumwood's account suggests that these shadow places are the externalities of capitalist process – the outside of value. Such places support the high material status of many lives around the world, particularly in the West: 'the places that take our pollution and dangerous waste, that are exhausted by extraction or cleared for industrial production'. She draws upon Barbara Ehrenreich's critique of capitalist practice and the 'illusion of dematerialisation' that capitalism cultivates – the excision from view and cultural memory of the real, placed and embodied labours and impacts that the world's wealth relies upon.

These places are not just physical, they are psychic too. They are places detached from dominant imaginings of national identity and cultural value. Australian scholars have pointed to the origins of this practice in the act of colonisation itself: as the land is appropriated by settlement and white sovereignty claimed, the country's history as Aboriginal land is rendered *past*, as over. The edict of *terra nullius* went one step further and denied Indigenous presence, even as past. In both the physical and discursive practices of colonisation, the concept of 'year zero', as Deborah Bird Rose calls it in *Reports From a Wild Country* (2004), erased prior presence with the arrival of the frontier of colonisation, and was mobilised as the predicate of the Australian nation.

Even when the impacts of colonisation on Indigenous people and country are admitted in these practices, they are commonly framed as a problem in need of fixing – as something to repair, get over, and move on from. Australian political discourse over the twenty years since the *Mabo* decision and subsequent landmark reports on Indigenous disadvantage and governmental practice – such as the *Bringing Them Home: The 'Stolen Generations' Report* (1997) – has advanced the sentiment that Australia needs to 'get over' and clean up its unsettling pasts in order to progress as a nation. Former Prime Minister Howard's attack on 'black armband history', for example, is indicative of this, as is the claim of Justices Deane and Gaudron. In their *Mabo* judgement, quoted in Frank Brennan, *One Land, One Nation* (1995), they stated that '[t]he nation as a whole must remain diminished unless and until there is an acknowledgement of, and *retreat* from, those past injustices' (emphasis added).

Yet as cultural historians continually remind us, the past cannot be put so easily aside. It continues its effects in untimely ways. Ross Gibson articulates this powerfully in his book *Seven Versions of an Australian Badland* (2002), where he writes that 'history lives as a presence in the landscape, a presence generated as a forceful outcome of countless actions, wishes and wills…People upon people, land upon landscape. Past upon present and future'. The 'badlands' in Gibson's account spatialise our cultural tendency to put 'outside' those histories that do not suit our vision of ourselves: these are places 'where evil can be banished so that goodness can be credited, by contrast, in the regions all around'.

This returns us to Plumwood's article and the capitalist fantasy Ehrenreich captures: 'to be cleaned up after…to achieve a certain magical weightlessness and immateriality' – to be untethered by history. While remediation or the address of injustice may be the goal of a discourse that seeks to 'move on' from the past, the problem with desiring historical distance from damage implicitly removes that damage from a proximity that would mean an ongoing engagement with its significance. It would assert that those things that unsettle us can be singularly addressed and put aside and that they have no place in the present.

The consequences of this kind of spatial and psychic quarantining is the continued marginalisation of the already socially marginal and disadvantaged, and the perpetuation of a national identity that continues a colonial vision of passive land, linear time and certain claim to place, and with it the colonising practices that lay waste to so much. It endorses the refusal to take responsibility for what is consigned to the badlands; it erases the shadows from our places.

Plumwood's message is that we cannot pick and choose the places that are meaningful to us. Every place has in its composition the imprint of other places. Just as the impact of events radiate, so too, with places. Let's return to the Mallee. In Plumwood's account, we can see the drought-plagued, deforested Mallee as a shadow place of the well-watered and strongly built city of Melbourne. The wealth in its architecture and its ever-burgeoning boundaries speak silently of the other places that fuelled and sustained its development.

This kind of foundational account of place, however – putting the Mallee/Melbourne relationship within an account of cause and effect, for instance – doesn't really capture the dynamism with which places shadow and entangle in the other. To recover this multidimensionality, we need to look to the fluid, rather than determined, nature of this relationship, to its constant enactment. And we need to look to the atmosphere.

Even as I type, smoke from regional bushfires blankets Melbourne's CBD and its inner suburbs. These fires have been burning in the Latrobe Valley and East Gippsland, and in outer suburbs to the north of the city. Our atmosphere is full of these minglings that are temporal, material and not always visible. They are minglings that disturb the fixed locations of place on a map; they bring different happenings, weathers and environments into relationship with each other. Here, in my Melbourne home, with the light differently refracted through a hazy sky, and the smell of burnt vegetation, animals and homes around me, I am in a place that is not just here, but somewhere else, too. It is a place that refuses to ignore or excise the experiences and histories that have produced this atmosphere.

Lake Tyrrell in Melbourne: Postcolonial atmospheres

Melbourne's air is always host to different minglings, some more toxic than others. In October 1956, for instance, a radioactive cloud passed across the city, having already moved through the air of Adelaide on its way from Maralinga, the site of the secret British atomic testing program. Given the unpredictable nature of radiation, which is elastic and non–linear in its dispersal and effects, what invisible traces of this cloud remain left behind in the wake of history? A different sort of cloud that has repeatedly visited Melbourne is the topsoil blown south from the dry Mallee and adjacent Wimmera lands, which turn the air brown and at times have moved with such force that the earth from these places has travelled as far as Tasmania.

Such minglings matter because they are the basis of what I call a 'postcolonial atmosphere'. This is an opportunity to recover diverse terrains of value, and in so doing, imagine our selves differently, through an always–negotiated relationship with place. An atmosphere is a condition of possibility. It is an air of emergence. It is also, as Peter Sloterdijk writes in 'Atmospheric Politics' (2005), a 'shared climate', something fundamental to democratic process and the extension of political franchise and the decentralisation of value. For me, a *postcolonial* atmosphere is one in which the divisions and represssions of colonial practice are challenged by the entanglements of a place always open to elsewhere, where the past constantly solicits us in the present, and we are continually proximate to the experiences of others.

In such an atmosphere, damage and the 'wastes' of colonialisation and its ongoing iteration become points of relation rather than disconnection. They open up place rather than closing it off, and highlight the webs of responsibility and connection that lace through the shadow network of lives and environments in our shiny modern cities. But an atmosphere is not all about the air, it is about the ground too; it is about the multidimensions of habitation. This returns us to Federation Square and the presence of Lake Tyrrell in swirls of pink sandstone.

Nearamnew, by my fellow Mallee traveller Paul Carter, is an artwork that comprises the plaza floor of Federation Square. It depicts the whorling form of a flooding Lake Tyrrell – an unlikely event now – in a large-scale ground design of 7,500 square metres that references the different histories of the lake and its Mallee environs. Different hues and patterns of stone trace out Lake Tyrrell in an image derived by Carter from a nineteenth-century Wergaia (an Indigenous language group whose country took in the Lake Tyrrell area) bark etching now housed in the National Gallery of Victoria.

Within *Nearamnew*'s Lake Tyrrell waters are more local histories of water, with the flowing stones incorporating nine 'rents' or boxes of carved text, which network together, recalling the system of local creeks and waterholes that, before colonial intervention, once fed into what is now the Yarra River flowing alongside Federation Square. Within these boxes are poetic texts composed by Carter that are drawn from an assemblage of stories in the margins of the historical archive. These include stories of Indigenous peoples and ecologies, and postcolonial meetings; stories of workers, of women and of children; stories of other places, of visitors and of migrants. These poetic texts are written into the marbled sandstone and are only partially legible, meaning that those who pass through the Square will always encounter the artwork differently, and incompletely, in snatches of variant words and shapes. These fleeting encounters between the artwork and its visitors take place via both the eye and the feet; they are embodied and poetic. They are also more than a single moment of meeting in a particular place and time. The histories that lace through here lead us elsewhere, to other spaces and happenings that we can never wholly know or access, but to which we always bear some relation. *Nearamnew* reminds us of, while it also enacts, this profoundly postcolonial condition.

On 13 February 2008, thousands of people gathered across the whorls of Lake Tyrrell in Federation Square to hear Prime Minister Rudd make an apology on behalf of the Parliament of Australia to the many victims of the country's stolen generations. Satellites beamed the centre of Australian political power into Federation Square, and linked its crowd to similar gatherings in many locations across the country. Rudd's speech called on non-Indigenous Australians to connect through their imaginations to the experience of Indigenous Australians injured in multiple ways by colonial practices: to empathically engage with the experiences of its victims. Yet it is not simply a matter of choosing to connect. The dynamic contact between feet and ground on that day – as on others – at Federation Square asks us to register a fundamental aspect of an atmosphere: its inescapability. We can tell neither where it begins nor ends. We are always swept up in its unfolding.

Non-Indigenous Australians do not stand outside colonial atmospheres, they are always and already within them absolutely, and the presence of Lake Tyrrell at Federation Square enacts this fact. Here is more than a representational form of the lake and its Mallee surrounds. It is an iteration of the Lake in its various histories. It is part of its existence and its coming into being. The Mallee dust that sometimes settles over the form of Lake Tyrrell at Federation Square re-performs this relation, reminding us that rural histories are also urban histories – the practices that have eroded environments in south-eastern Australia's agricultural lands reach far into the city spaces, with their linear grids and urban planning frameworks.

If we are always caught up in colonial atmospheres, though, how to transform them, how to become postcolonial? I return to the Mallee poet John Shaw Neilson, who guided our Mallee trip. He wrote the poem 'Stony Town' when he visited Melbourne, and it offers a lament for the loss of ecology as Melbourne sought to transform itself into a modern metropolis. Neilson's picture of Stony Town is one of 'straight line[s]' and 'square[s]' and hard, unforgiving surfaces. The city's reality is blunt, we are told – 'It buys and sells and buys'. And yet even here there is a third dimension, located in the shadow place of dreams: 'The bells will laugh and the men will laugh, and the girl shall shine so fair/With the scent of love and cinnamon dust shaken out of her hair/Her skirts shall be of the gossamer, full thirty inches high/And her lips shall move as the flowers move to see the wind go by'. Within these stony urban surrounds Neilson could still discern the other histories to remember. The mobile air, mutable and full of the possible, remains.

Postcolonial atmospheres intersect as possibilities with the disconnecting, alienating enactments of colonial power that continue to damage our environments and peoples. They blow in from our shadow places and engulf our daily movements around spatial, social and economic boundaries. In a context of community stress, and the connected challenges of environments that cannot sustain the lives we would like to lead, a shift in perspective is needed wherein the 'waste' of progress is reconsidered rather than rejected. Histories are our resources: these shadow realities brought into the realm of daily encounter are our assets. Opening our selves and our places up to this reorientation expands the range of value by which we assess and know what matters, and within this, negotiate an ethical footing in place: a belonging that doesn't degrade but revitalises our communities and environments.

Indigeneity and the Archive: Mediating the Public, the Private and the Communal

Miranda Johnson

> In every community that manages to sustain or revive itself over time, there are cultural factors that contribute to the vitality and robustness of the people living there. These factors are shared and creative, which is to say they are cultural and they are assets that make life valuable, that make life worth living.
>
> Ross Gibson, 'What Is a Cultural Asset?'

In this chapter, I map out an argument for the importance of the archive as a cultural asset. I propose that the archive is a particular kind of asset, since 'archive' is both a noun and a verb. As a noun, archive denotes most simply a storehouse or repository of texts (written, visual, audio, and digital) that have public value. As a verb, *to* archive refers to the action of storing such texts somewhere, or even the action of recording itself (I will return to the idea of recording later). Moreover, one archives something for the purpose of building something larger, a *collection* of texts that are greater than the sum of the parts. This collection is to be preserved *for* someone or something: a nation; or a local community such as a shire or a tribe; and even for those who don't yet exist – future generations. The archive is both a cultural asset in itself, and it refers to the action of creating such an asset; it is something already ascribed value by those who fund it and work in it, and it is something that creates value for those who use it.

I am particularly interested in how archives mediate the overlapping worlds of the public, the personal and the communal. Let me begin by distinguishing these terms in relation to the archive. I mentioned previously that the archive is a repository of texts considered to have value for the public. What is this public? In a somewhat circular fashion, the public is a group or readership who we imagine to hold a potential or extant interest in the archive, for instance because the archive contains texts about the proceedings of government bodies that represent that public. In other words, the public is imagined to already exist by virtue of what the archival collection is about and, at the same time, the public is brought into existence through the act of defining what is included or excluded from the archive. This public is somewhat anonymous and could be or become quite diverse over time; not everyone who constitutes this public is known to each other, although they may all claim citizenship, for example, to the same country.

The public value of the archive is made meaningful through the personal engagements of individuals with texts in the actual site of the archive. These personal engagements with the archive might be daunting, revelatory, or even painful – for archivist and client alike. Hence, the archive becomes a site of encounter between the personal history of the individual and the text object found in the archival collection. The text object was acquired because it was considered to have a public value, but it is only in the personal interaction between, say, text and reader that such a value becomes really meaningful. In encountering the text in the archive, the individual may then contest its public value – such as its truthfulness – as we shall see later in the chapter.

Finally, the archive can serve an idea and practice of com- munity – that is, a group of people defined by something they share beyond a broadly held political or economic interest such as shared descent, or attachment to a particular place, or other kinds of emotional bonds. Archives can serve to help us understand our sense of *belonging* to each other, or to a place. And they can shore up ideas or feelings about who doesn't belong and why. Archives, as we shall see, can become key sites in (re)establishing a community. By collecting texts that have a particular meaning for a distinct community, archivists can help to frame how members of a community understand the ways in which they belong together. This framework for belonging may be quite different from how a larger public imagines itself as citizens in a state; and the community archive may even limit how much of the archive is available to that broader public in the interest of maintaining community norms and customs over and above what the public thinks it is entitled to view.

In this chapter, I discuss the ways that archives mediate the public, the personal, and the communal in reference to the representation of Indigenous peoples in archives and their engagements with those institutional collections. Archives are important sites for the revitalisation of Indigenous communities and cultures; yet archives of the state in particular have been formed through processes of colonisation that have certainly not served Indigenous peoples' interests or needs well. Nonetheless, today Indigenous peoples use archives to reconnect with family members, locate ethnographic information about their communities from historical accounts, map out tribal territories, and so on. Even more significantly, as I turn to at the end of the essay, Indigenous communities have created their own archives, to serve the needs and interests of their members, and even to establish and assert a sense of their own community. The stories that I will tell in brief here about indigeneity and the archive are quite particular and yet I think these stories also have something to tell other communities – particularly ones seeking to sustain and revive themselves in a context of economic downturn or the loss of population, in order to make life for their members worth living, as Ross Gibson puts it.

Archives and public value

The documents and other materials stored in archives are ascribed a value that is considered by whomever makes the decision to acquire them to be one that goes beyond the individual archivist's own interests. In other words, the 'public' value of the archival collection is (at least implicitly) distinguished from the 'private' value that might be ascribed by an individual according to his or her subjective ideas of something's worth. The public value of an archive is something that the individual archivist, and the archival organisation that they represent, thinks is important for others: the broader (though anonymous) members of a public.

This public value is usually described in the mission statements and acquisition objectives stated by archival institutions. However, individual archives will frame what they think the public finds of value in their collections differently. Therefore, what kind of 'public' is imagined as a consequence is distinctive in each case. The National Archives of Australia (NAA), for example, explains that it is responsible for 'accepting, preserving and making Commonwealth records of archival value accessible for current and future generations'. Obviously, the NAA does not mean that records worthy of archiving are made accessible for *all* generations, everywhere around the world. In more refined selection objectives, the NAA's website, 'Why Records Are Kept – Directions in Appraisal', explains that its selection criteria include preserving evidence of Commonwealth government activities, particularly those that contain 'information that is considered essential for the protection and future well-being of Australians and their environment'. The public that the NAA imagines is a national public, one to whom, in a representative democracy, the Commonwealth government is responsible and that therefore has a right to access what the government does in its name.

The State Library of New South Wales, which houses the Mitchell Library, has broader 'heritage' goals, which are defined geographically and historically rather than politically. As stated in the library's 'Collection Development Policy', the original remit for the Mitchell Library, composed in 1910 – following the bequest by the Sydney bibliophile David Scott Mitchell – was to collect materials from 'a geographical area embracing Australia and all places north to the Philippines and Hawaii, south to the Antarctic, east to Easter Island and west to Sumatra, all inclusive but excluding the mainlands of Asia, Africa and the Americas and the islands adjacent to them'. The library explains its historical goals thus: 'to document the development of Australia from the time New South Wales *was* substantially Australia and to create a collection that reflects the cultural heritage of New South Wales in both the Australian and international contexts'. The State Library thus defines the public value of its collections in terms of the historical importance of New South Wales (NSW) as the first of the Australian colonies, and in terms of its Oceanic as well as more local collections. Thus, the State Library explains its benefit to NSW residents in cultural and social terms.

Just because an archival collection is ascribed public value does not mean that all records are publicly available. Particularly sensitive state records may be embargoed for a certain number of years; and sometimes individual donations are made under the condition that records cannot be viewed until the donor has died, or gives their personal permission for them to be viewed. So, access to the archive is limited in key ways: by the definition of the public to whom and for whom the archive is responsible (as a nation, or as consumers and producers of cultural heritage); and also by what can and should be made available, when, and to whom (according to those who deposit the records). Even if the archive is considered to have public value, not everything in it is publicly available.

The public value of archives itself may change, as use of certain collections changes. Fifty years ago, those accessing the NAA records would mainly have been government bureaucrats and political historians. Now the records are accessed by a wide variety of Australians (and non-Australians). The NAA's website has helpful tips for those carrying out family history, or genealogical research, for instance. The State Library of NSW has probably always had a more diverse clientele. In her David Scott Mitchell Memorial Lecture, 'Hunters and Gatherers: A Novelist's Debt to the Mitchell Library', given in 2010, the novelist Kate Grenville applauded the welcoming atmosphere of the library, 'where any old person can wander in off the street, and frequently does. Wander in, sit down, and read the books freely available on the open shelves'. Nonetheless, the State Library now actively encourages 'informal' users and children and, according to its chief executive, is now rebuilding itself as a 'Global Library for a Global City'. Digitisation projects that all libraries and archives are undertaking encourage use and engagement by an even broader, and more diverse, clientele.

The archives of the state, some would say, have undergone a kind of democratisation in the sense that they are now accessed by a range of people from different social and economic backgrounds, not just by elites with ready access to power. The value of such assets therefore changes over time, in the sense that a more diverse 'public' may now value archives for what they can help them find out about their own personal histories as well as about the history of the state. Of course, this doesn't necessarily make entering a large, state-sponsored archive less of a daunting, even alienating experience. Texts that contain information about you or your family or someone or something you are interested in will be catalogued according to systems that are not readily familiar, and will remain so until you have spoken with an archivist, searched online, and begun to make sense of the order in which they have been placed.

What I think is quite remarkable about archives, even large state ones like the NAA, is that, despite the forbiddingness of many archive buildings and the technical knowledge that must be acquired in order to access files, the encounter with a text in this context can be deeply personal. In amongst the quiet page-turning of the reading room, a giggle might escape your lips; you might tingle with the euphoria of discovery. Sometimes what you are looking for has been lost, or is in a state of disrepair, which means you can't access it and this can be profoundly frustrating. Even what you find is likely only a fragment of what you had hoped for. And what you might find can be shocking, upsetting, unnerving. Maybe even that fragment is too much to bear in the moment of reading. Thus, the personal enters the archive, encounters the archival collections, and may even change or contest what is publicly valuable about that collection.

Contesting the archive: The personal versus official

In the Introduction to *Wherever I Go: Myles Lalor's 'Oral History'* (2000), anthropologist Jeremy Beckett recalls what provoked Lalor into wanting to record his 'oral history':

> One evening in 1987, Myles Lalor, an Aboriginal man I had known for almost thirty years, came around to my house in Sydney…He had spent the day looking up his personal files in the archives of the old Aborigines Welfare Board, and what he had found had left him angry and upset. Although the documents were more than forty years old, he felt defamed…Suddenly, and to my surprise, since we had never discussed such a possibility before, he said, 'I think you'd better do my oral history'.

Lalor, Beckett writes in the introduction, felt that his reputation had been defamed, or slandered, on account of the false statements he read about himself in the personal files of the Aboriginal Welfare Board. These statements referred to his time as a youth in the Kinchela Aboriginal Boys' Training Home in New South Wales and made, according to Lalor, 'outrageous' claims about him. Yet, because of the impersonal administrative tone they were likely written in, and the fact that Lalor located them in archives associated with the state, they bore the value of factual truth. In order to counter this 'truth', and put the record straight, Lalor decided that he must record his version of his story, in case, as he said to his daughter, 'in a hundred years, somebody pick[s] up that file and start[s] looking back.' (When Lalor encountered the file, it was available only to his family and even Beckett himself did not see it when recording and then editing Lalor's oral history.)

This first motivation for recording his version of his life's story is a public, even political one. Lalor wanted to produce a kind of 'counter-archive' that would contest the purported 'truth' of the official archive and, in order to do so, he had to publish – that is, make public – a better account, one that was a much fuller and indeed more lively story of his own life. In order to do so, he strategically chose a well-known and highly respected anthropologist who also knew him well to carry out the work. There is an interesting ethical practice at work here, for in so doing, Lalor placed the obligation for publication on the man to whom he had provided material. It is one that, as I have argued, some donators to public archives also enact when they embargo certain materials or put access to those materials under certain limitations or restrictions.

The edited text was published in 2000, a full twelve years after Lalor died, mainly, it seems, because of the time it took Beckett to transcribe and edit the complicated stories that Lalor recorded, sometimes in the presence of Beckett or his own sister, and sometimes by himself, with no listeners present. It is a poignant, sometimes bitter, wry and subtle account of his life, of travelling and working mainly around the small towns of the NSW outback, from Uralla (or 'Struggletown…as long as I've lived, it's always been referred to as Struggletown') to Kinchela, to Redfern, out to Cunnamulla, up the Birdsville Track, and down to Wilcannia. The story of a life's journey, expressed in a strong personal voice, is itself a kind of archive – supplemented in the book by photos of Lalor, his friends and relatives, as well as maps of his travels, and a genealogy. It is certainly more public than whatever was contained in the Aboriginal Welfare Board records. And it is a publication, we might say, that puts the heart back into the record of a human life.

Indeed, the etymology of 're-cord' takes us back to the Greek for heart, καρδία. The first meaning given to 'record' in the Oxford English Dictionary is to 'learn by heart'. This meaning was overtaken by another in the eighteenth century – a period in which the written record became more important as evidence in courts of law – to mean that of setting down in writing something told or remembered orally. According to the French philosopher and historian Michel de Certeau, the shift in the West to writing and away from a mostly oral culture was a transformation in the service of capitalism and colonialism in which writing and orality were imbued with different ideological values. In *The Practice of Everyday Life* (trans. 1984), de Certeau writes: 'the "oral" is that which does not contribute to progress; reciprocally, the "scriptural" is that which separates itself from the magical world of voices and tradition'. Nonetheless, the 'oral' sensibility – in this example, Myles Lalor's oral history, composed to counter an official archive – is precisely what is so powerful about what is given to us on the page.

The highly personal tone of Lalor's story and its oral sensibility reveals not only that 'orality' survives the onslaught of a written culture, but it also leads us to think about the urge entailed in all kinds of recording. As Beckett points out in his afterword to the book, there was probably more going on for Lalor in recording his oral history than countering the official archive. Lalor, Beckett suggests, apprehended a danger, one of an existential nature. He was worried about what would survive of his life once he died: as Beckett puts it, he feared that 'with his death the self he sustained through his traveller's tales would disintegrate'. Thus, Lalor was perhaps urged on to *preserve* his story in order to defy the disintegration that death brings about. In this sense the possibility of making a story public is about more than 'truth'; it is about the survival of the person after death. This urge, moreover, is perhaps what lies at the heart of all archival projects: that something about each one of us, whether deeply personal or even mundane, will leave an imprint that future generations will respond to, care for, and hopefully cherish.

Creative community archives: The Mulka Project

This yearning for preservation and survival is particularly sharp for communities that have not been well served by public archives and official history-writing in the past. Moreover, in the age of the digital, the possibilities for more dynamic, interactive and expansive archives are greater than ever before. Indeed, the possibilities that digitisation and access to digital resources offer make the vista of the infinite-yet-total library in Jorge Luis Borges' *The Library of Babel* (trans. 2000) an aspiration shared by librarians themselves, as I noted previously: the idea of a 'global library for a global city'. Strikingly, digital archives are also something around which local communities have begun to organise themselves. As digitisation projects, and the storing of digital material, opens up a vista of a global clientele, the digital archive is also playing a significant role in cohering local communities, and providing a locus point for imagining themselves into the future.

The Mulka Project is a Yolngu initiative and it is both a production house and digital archive that, as its website explains, aims to 'sustain and protect Yolngu cultural knowledge in Northeast Arnhem Land' (see http://www.mulka.org/themulkaproject/about). The term 'mulka' refers to a sacred and public ceremony, and can be glossed as 'hold, take hold of, touch, feel, grab, reach, arrive at'. Like the term 'archive', the term 'mulka' describes something and does something. The concept crosses the overlapping ways I have discussed regarding the archive: the process of archiving, and engagement with archives. I like the way the term embraces notions of holding and grabbing, as well as tactility, and the idea of having arrived somewhere, perhaps at the end of a long search. Or maybe the idea of arriving can also remind us that arriving somewhere may only be a temporary condition, a time for pause and replenishment before beginning another journey.

Significantly, the creators of the Mulka Project distinguish between the value of the archive to the immediate community it serves – that is, Yolngu people – and a wider public. In the first instance, the archive is being developed in order to sustain Yolngu knowledge and culture within Yolngu communities. The goals of the digital archive project are to benefit and enhance the lives of local people themselves, by providing employment and training, access to the Internet, and the preservation of cultural material. The Mulka directors intend to repatriate material from around Australia and even from around the world – photographs, films and so on – that involve and represent Yolngu people and places over the past century, by bringing it back to the facilities in Yirrkala village. This historical material can then be used to inform contemporary productions, including contemporary dance and music videos and animations.

Public (that is, non-Yolngu) access to the archives is permitted, though the availability of material is subject to Yolngu law and governance structures. This is a common restriction that Indigenous communities place on access to cultural material and knowledge by outsiders. (Even inside communities there may be limitations or law prohibiting access to some material depending on gender, age or status.) Such restrictions, while frustrating perhaps to outsiders, are important mechanisms for asserting the community's norms and expectations. In other words, even the ways in which such archives can be used and accessed can work to 'sustain and revive' culture by putting into practice the cultural frameworks by which particular communities abide. Such norms and expectations – sometimes but not always expressed in explicit regulations – also frame large public archives such as the National Archives of Australia. As I mentioned earlier, those archives may contain collections considered too sensitive to be made publicly available. Or they may contain personal information that institutions have now decided should be available only to those about whom the information was composed. As well as such explicit regulations, archives are bound by social norms, such as what is considered important to citizens of a democracy, or residents of a state territory. These values may change over time, and such change itself indicates the importance and vitality of such cultural institutions.

Conclusion

In this chapter, I have argued that the archive is an important cultural asset. I have suggested this is so because of the way the archive mediates plural groups and interests: that is, the way it maintains and even creates value for a broad but anonymous national public, for individuals (even where individuals may want to contest what they find about themselves in the archive), and for communities seeking to sustain and revive themselves. Archives are both repositories of cultural value, and they help us to produce cultural value. The texts stored in archives inspire us to tell stories about ourselves, who we are and where we come from. They might provoke us to contest a public image of who others think we are. They encourage us to imagine otherwise, to engage with texts and hence imaginations that are very different from our own, even those which might recognisably belong to the same place we call home. Documents stored in archives thus help us to pose counter-factuals and establish differences: we might be prompted to think about who we are *not*, and how different we are from those who actually created the texts – including written documents, photographs, films and so on – in the past. I have argued that the very ways in which archives are instituted reflects and can further establish cultural and social value through the norms and expectations that are embedded in what is collected, how it is stored, and how access to that material is made available and to whom. Finally, I have even suggested that we *need* archives in an existential sense, in order to counter the otherwise ephemeral sense that once we are dead, the life that we lived disintegrates.

Locating the Local:
Culture, Place and the Citizen

Deborah Stevenson

Much has been written about the benefits that supposedly flow to those cities and regions that put culture and applied creativity at the centre of their place-making and community development strategies. Overwhelmingly, the focus of this writing is positive, suggesting that such approaches have the potential to generate activity, be the impetus for the growth of new industries and revitalise urban space. There are a number of factors driving the interest in culture-led city reimaging and development, including substantial challenges to local economies resulting most recently from the global financial crisis, emerging forms of leisure and retailing, the growth of new technologies and changes in the nature of manufacturing that have led to deindustrialisation and abandonment in numerous cities and regions around the world. Warehouses and factories stand empty; many town and city centres no longer perform the people- and activity-based functions they once did and, as a result, shops and offices have closed. And even those cities that may not have suffered a serious economic downturn will contain within them rundown or abandoned precincts that were once the thriving spaces of production or consumption.

The starting point for any consideration of culture-led urban planning and development (cultural planning) is to observe the pervasiveness of local strategies designed to use the arts and 'culture' to achieve a range of urban, social, creative and economic ends. Most of these blueprints pivot on a rather predictable suite of recommendations and, while underpinning each strategy is invariably an economic agenda of self-sufficiency or revival, a number of other themes are also evident in relation to this goal. Innovation, sustainability and knowledge are three relatively recent additions to the discourses of cultural planning, but enduring within most plans and approaches are three interconnected ingredients – culture/creativity, citizenship and place – that are frequently the touchstones of cultural planning and the vehicles for achieving a range of objectives.

Despite contradictory ideas and political contexts there has been a remarkably uniform set of pronouncements for positioning and interpreting culture within city-based cultural planning, and in this respect although the pivotal influences are diffuse and often paradoxical, the discursive shift from 'art' to 'culture' is central. Conceptions of an urban citizen and the existence of a democratic public realm are also fundamental to cultural planning. The idea of citizenship is played out most interestingly through the discourses of 'the civic', 'cosmopolitanism' and 'social inclusion' and although each theme is discrete they contribute in different ways to a view of the citizen as active and locally engaged. In addition, at the core of the cultural planning notion of urban citizenship is a conception of the 'new' middle/cultural/creative class that is understood in terms of aesthetics, taste and, most significantly, the ability to consume. Indeed, the pursuit of economic development and participation in the urban economy is frequently considered central to the achievement of social inclusion and local citizenship.

Cultural planning is also implicitly and explicitly about place. This is a concern that takes many forms, however. For instance, as well as seeking to create places that are meaningful to local people, cultural planning is also concerned with marketing place and positioning place-identity as part of broader city branding and reimaging strategies. Not uncommonly, however, it is the places of the inner city that are the focus of such initiatives which frequently involve gentrification and building specialist cultural and tourist precincts. Other parts of the city, in particular the suburbs where most people live, are the frequent silences of these place-making and branding strategies, while the situation (and applicability) of cultural planning to places within towns and regions beyond the metropolis is vexed and uneven. The aim of this chapter is briefly to trace the contours of these influential themes and to reflect on their consequences for the local.

Frames of culture

It seems somewhat redundant to say that culture is at the heart of cultural planning and associated strategies designed to position a city as 'creative'. But as is well established within academic fields such as cultural studies, culture is one of the most complex concepts in contemporary social and cultural theory and this complexity takes shape within cultural planning. A key initiative of early exponents of cultural planning was to challenge the established priorities of arts organisations and move away from an understanding of culture as 'art' – a set of identifiable works and practices that are associated with excellence – to embrace a broader suite of activities and products from the popular and technological to the everyday and the local. In *The Long Revolution* (1965), Raymond Williams describes a tripartite characterisation of culture as referring to a particular way of life as well as to artistic works and activities, and processes of 'intellectual, spiritual and aesthetic development'. This definitional nuance was both influential and useful in providing a justification for broadening the scope from arts to cultural policy and the 'anthropological' definition of culture as a way of life that gained currency in cultural studies was quickly adopted within cultural planning. The shift has not been seamless, however, and definitional inconsistencies abound.

Cultural plans may be couched in the language of an all-embracing view of culture as a way of life and much is often made of the importance of meaning, belief, memory and ritual, but the actual plans are all too often concerned with a fairly traditional – frequently elite – suite of 'arts' practices and products. Similar tensions between competing understandings of culture are also apparent in the city culture initiatives of many national arts funding bodies, such as those of the National Endowment for the Arts in the United States, and of Australia's peak arts funding body, the Australia Council, which have in different ways been active in promoting cultural planning and in turn influencing the priorities and focus of local programs. For instance, the Our Town program of the National Endowment for the Arts – in spite of its focus on revitalisation, liveability and 'community spirit' – is nevertheless principally concerned with providing support for arts and cultural facilities.

Expanding what counts as culture to include popular forms and commodities has also involved establishing a language for asserting the economic value and contribution of the arts and the cultural sector to localities. This expansion has in turn made it possible to shift the focus away from a subsidy approach to arts policy to one that emphasises industry development and incubation. However, as Justin O'Connor points out in his paper 'The Cultural and Creative Industries' (2013), there are considerable tensions between conceptualisations of the 'cultural industries' and the related notion of 'creative industries' that find expression in urban cultural policy and planning. In broad terms the creative industries discourse tends to privilege the contribution of creativity and talent to wealth development and in this respect economic ends are dominant. A 'cultural industries' approach, on the other hand – at least as it was initially framed – is concerned with promoting the use of economic resources to foster community cultural development and processes of local democracy. The cultural/creative industries debate is one that continues apace at least within academic circles but it is probably fair to say that in spite of differences in their founding principles and occasionally in their application, the two terms have largely come to be used interchangeably in practice.

Along with broadening the definition of what counts as culture and the assertion of a cultural/creative industries agenda, cultural planning also has a pivotal and more nuanced concern with the idea of creativity and the creative – cultural planning is in many ways promoted as a means of producing 'creative cities'. Creativity in this context often assumes some of the definitional breadth afforded to culture. But creativity is also about particular qualities – of place, residents and ways of thinking. It relates to innovation, imagination and energy. It is coded texture and vitality. Thus the idea of creativity is very seductive particularly when combined with the promise of economic development, which goes some way towards explaining why cities have been quick to embrace a creativity agenda.

Cultural planning is often also concerned with the way in which governments at different levels support the field of community arts. In the 1960s and 1970s, the philosophical justification for community arts policies and programs emerged in the dominant aesthetic discourse that produced two categories of subject: those who recognised and appreciated 'art' and those who did not. The groups that subsequently were identified became the constituency or client group of community arts programs, and the creative practices that were selected for endorsement were those deemed to express the collective identity of a group rather than the artistic mastery of particular individuals. The 'communities' that were positioned as being 'outside' (or marginalised by) the dominant aesthetic paradigms were those deemed to be culturally or socially 'disadvantaged'.

The development of cultural planning challenged the principles of disadvantage that lay at the heart of community arts, prompting a reconceptualisation that found later expression in the discourses of social exclusion and inclusion. Cultural planning provided the policy context for a reworking of community arts and in some countries provoked a shifting of responsibility for access and equity from national arts funding bodies to state and/ or local governments. It also established the groundwork for a rethinking of cultural democracy and social justice in relation to cultural policy that, in turn, was centrally about a particular conceptualisation of the citizen. Expansive conceptualisations of culture have made possible the definitional space for adopting an expansive approach to cultural planning, and central to this agenda is cultural planning as a tool for fostering local citizenship.

Forming the citizen

There are three prominent dimensions of citizenship invoked within cultural planning – the civic, cosmopolitanism and social inclusion. Initially, cultural planning as a tool to build local citizens had foundations within the British Labour Party, which embedded in cultural planning the importance of the civic (as a physical and political space) and the provision of public spaces and cultural facilities in the 'civic heart' of the city. But directly and indirectly this agenda has also come to support entrepreneurial and city-imaging strategies often focused on consumption. The citizen conceived in terms of the civic has become one that is constituted principally in the public and quasi-public precincts of the (gentrified) inner city and, in spite of being couched in the language of democracy and community, is in fact highly individualised, mobile and middle-class.

In this context, the idea of cosmopolitanism has become particularly relevant, emerging in recent years to be a key dimension of cultural planning and its invocation of the citizen. 'Cosmopolitan citizenship' is both a contradictory notion and shaped through a number of seemingly incongruous but, nevertheless, intersecting discourses including, in particular, those associated with Richard Florida's idea of the 'creative class' and the 'intercultural' city, as described by Phil Wood and Charles Landry (2008). Citizenship imagined in terms of cosmopolitanism also speaks to themes of the global which are not only in tension with a conception of citizenship framed in terms of the civic and the city, but also with the local and the third dimension of the way in which cultural planning evokes themes of citizenship – social inclusion.

As I explain in '"Civic Gold" Rush: Cultural Planning and the Politics of the Third Way' (2004), citizenship expressed in terms of social inclusion is most evident in cultural strategies and programs that have been developed to give marginal(ised) groups the opportunity to participate fully in society and by extension become 'active' citizens. Social inclusion is often understood as being something of a synonym for social justice, which was an original aim of both community arts initiatives and British cultural planning. However, the two have very different objectives and are grounded in very different ideological assumptions, with social inclusion being focused on providing individuals with opportunities to be active citizens while social justice is concerned with outcomes and communities. What is also pivotal is that the achievement of social inclusion through cultural planning is often premised on an engagement in the cultural economy.

Bodies that have the international or transnational rather than the local or national as their concern have also adopted strategies that influence, and are influenced by, cultural planning. In varying ways, such programs must nevertheless also negotiate the local and national and associated ideas of citizenship. The Capitals of Culture program of the European Union is perhaps the highest profile attempt by an international body to intervene in, and support, the cultural agenda of cities as a strategy for fostering transnational dialogue and integration. The European Capitals of Culture program seeks to promote the local, while at the same time speak to themes of European-ness and the development of a pan-European sense of identity, disrupting, in a small way, taken-for-granted notions of citizenship.

In tandem with the language of citizenship expressed through the discourses of creativity, social inclusion and economic development, the idea of place and the goal of forging a sense of belonging and community through place-making and place animation are also fundamental to the rhetoric and objectives of cultural planning.

Making place

Place, the realm of the symbolic and the meaningful, speaks to themes of belonging, community and identity, and creative city/cultural planning strategies have at their core a concern with place-making and cultural mapping which, in the first instance, is focused on the emotive and representational. In order to implement such strategies, however, it is necessary to flatten or abbreviate place, summarising its meanings and resonances because, although the concern of cultural planning is with the complexity of place, it is often in the service of a strategy that is focused on place-marketing and city-imaging. I would further argue that the interest in place that has become dominant in cultural planning is underpinned by three factors. First, the cultural as everyday is often played out through the discourses of place – place provides a way for cultural policy and planning to engage with everyday life and meaning and thus is a discursive technique for moving beyond creative objects and activities. Second, the 'creative cities' focus that now dominates cultural planning puts place and the quality (and marketability) of the built environment at the centre of its strategies, and in this context major entertainment and redeveloped waterfront precincts are frequently to the fore. Third, the ambition to develop the creative/cultural industries through cultural planning leads to a concern with creating the spaces in which innovation and creativity, as well as creative businesses, can flourish. The making of cultural clusters, quarters, precincts and incubators are intended not only to develop the creative industries but also to animate and rehabilitate space – in other words, create place. These places can be permanent or temporary, embedded or fleeting, but they must always be populated and productive.

Beyond any tensions associated with delineating what is culture in cultural planning, most schemes are concerned with fostering or establishing places for the development of the cultural or creative industries. Many aim to create long-term spaces for creative workers – breeding grounds for successful businesses and the production of creative works. But many, too, are short-term and situational. Two examples are the 'pop-up' spaces that have become ubiquitous in the United Kingdom and the initiatives of Renew Newcastle and Renew Australia, which focus on the temporary occupation of abandoned buildings and shopfronts. At the other end of the spectrum is the establishment of large-scale cultural precincts, such as the West Kowloon Cultural District in Hong Kong and the Esplanade–Theatre on the Bay development in Singapore, which support high-profile cultural institutions. These and other initiatives are concerned with using the arts and culture as mechanisms for animating and making places. They aim to attract to a city or neighbourhood business, tourists, locals and of course, the 'creative class'. Urban vibrancy has become central to the lexicon of cultural planning and its place-making agenda as something that supposedly can be created as well as measured as an indicator of success.

Just as cultural planning is about place and situation, it is also about networks, connections and exchanges that shape the parameters of initiatives, frame core objectives and ensure the sharing and (invariable) copying of best practices. The role of consultants who travel the world to impart the secret of successful cultural planning and creative city-making is obvious. But there are still no clear and agreed upon methodologies for measuring the success or otherwise of cultural planning strategies, a point made often with respect to the status of Glasgow as the exemplar 'city of culture'. The absence of evidence, however, has not slowed the promotion and adoption of cultural planning around the world, often on the advice of those who have much to gain from the propagation of the idea.

The circulation of blueprints for urban cultural planning and development becomes complex when applied beyond the spaces and places of the metropolis to towns and regions because cultural planning has become strongly focused on cities and their cultures, places and citizens. This focus is evident within cultural planning even though its origins owe much to the regions, and its principles and processes have been applied beyond the metropolis. The cultures of everyday life are implicitly those of the urban; the practices and products of both the arts and the creative industries are overwhelmingly produced in the physical and imaginative spaces of the city. The cultural economy is routinely thought of as an urban one and the places and spaces of citizenship are similarly coded urban. The civic is implicitly urban, social inclusion speaks to themes of urban disadvantage and deviance, just as cosmopolitanism is about the spaces and dispositions of an urban elite, while the strategies of cultural planning, and its ambitions to foster a sense of belonging and identification, are often premised on the belief that it is possible to create/make place from anonymous urban space. For small towns and even provincial cities as the 'others' of cultural planning, the challenge and opportunities are profound even though deindustrialising regional cities and towns, such as Newcastle and Geelong in Australia and Liverpool and Newcastle-Gateshead in the United Kingdom, have been amongst the most eager to adopt culture-led recovery strategies. Indeed, it is also important not to lose sight of the pivotal role that northern regional cities played in the development of cultural planning in the United Kingdom. It is the case, therefore, that the relationship between urban and regional imaginaries in the discourses and practices of cultural planning are potent, contradictory and often highly political.

This point is illustrated by the example of the deindustrialising regional Australian city of Newcastle where, in the 1990s, a plan was formulated to change the negative image that the city was seen to have acquired because of its past as a centre for heavy industry. As I argue at length in the book *Cities and Urban Cultures*, pivotal to the strategy was a proposal to redevelop a large tract of the urban waterfront and to mark the regional port city both materially and symbolically as 'great'. In this quest, popular – indeed mythological – ideas about what such a city should look like were central to the redevelopment proposal put forward and to the public relations and media campaigns mobilised to gain local support for the proposal. It was explicitly claimed in the promotional literature that the redevelopment would see Newcastle take its place alongside the 'great port cities of the world' including London, Boston and Vancouver, as well as secure the city's economic, social and cultural futures. In other words, the redevelopment – with its focus on leisure, culture and consumption – was promoted as the trigger that would transform the image and appearance of the industrial city from that of a stigmatised, second-rate, 'coal town' into a vibrant and attractive 'great port city'.

The potency of this redevelopment proposal for local interest groups and residents came primarily from the symbolic status believed to accrue to cities that adopt particular reimaging strategies in response to the challenges of deindustrialisation. The existence of particular places and precincts is regarded as necessary for a city to gain a position somewhere within the global networks of cities – in this instance, the status of a 'great port city'. These networks mesh the economic with the political and the symbolic in a competitive game of attaining and retaining urban status. For a regional deindustrialising city, such status is intimately associated with the symbolism derived from the connectedness of the imagined and material forms of the metropolitan centres and the global status that certain landscapes are seen to announce.

Conclusion

The feel-good language of culture, place and citizenship, coupled with the hard-edged discourses of economic success and urban revitalisation create a compelling and intoxicating mix. Cities both metropolitan and provincial eagerly compete with each other on the basis of image, liveability, vitality and creativity, to name but four. They compete to receive official designations such as the European Capital of Culture, while asserting self-awarded labels such as 'Creative City Sydney' or Singapore's ambition to be a 'Renaissance City' and 'Global City for the Arts'.

The extent and scope of cultural planning is vast, and mapping its dimensions and concerns is challenging but necessary if it is to be understood and its potential harnessed. To this end, probing the thematic underpinnings of cultural planning is an important task. The arts and cultural industries are 'big business'; at the same time they are profoundly enmeshed in the everyday lives and concerns of people and their localities. They play a role in the expression and celebration of identity, and many commentators and arts administrators regard them as capable of civilising space and creating places that are lively, productive and meaningful. Cultural planning is something of a catch-all for strategies which, in different ways, seek to use the creative and cultural resources of a city as part of a broader agenda that is variously about fostering local democracy and citizenship, making and animating places, and supporting local economic development. It is simultaneously concerned with the cultural, social, urban and economic dimensions of everyday life. The fact that cultural planning rarely achieves the ambitions set for it has become somewhat incidental, if not irrelevant.

The extent to which cultural planning strategies and approaches can be transported from one place to another is also highly problematic and requires further investigation. Given its urban underpinning, there is also a clear need to consider exactly what cultural planning might productively mean in non-urban or even non-metropolitan contexts. The starting point must surely be 'the local', which means first finding a way to identify and then nurture local ways of life, forms of identification and engagements with place. Also necessary are robust measures of success. It is only by proceeding thus will it become possible to develop an informed and clearly framed cultural approach to the making and remaking of cities, towns and regions. This is an approach that is flexible and responsive and will support and nurture local cultures, places and forms of citizenship.

An earlier version of this chapter was published in D. Stevenson, *Cities of Culture: A Global Perspective,* Routledge, Abingdon, Oxon, 2014.

Speak Culture:
Culturised Planning for
Australia and the Globe

Greg Young

In *Speak, Memory* (1969), one of the great cosmopolitan novelists of the last century, Vladimir Nabokov, presents his autobiographical recollections of the culture of his early Russian life and times. The book's brusque title dramatises Nabokov's purpose and provides a resonant metaphor for the undertaking. I have long wished to see culture speak to Australia as potently as Nabokov's memory did to him. In particular, I have longed to see cultural knowledge and cultural understanding more consciously and effectively integrated into planning as its fundamental underpinning, with the ability to enrich all of the discipline's discourses and practices. In the last part of this chapter, I suggest one recent, forward-looking approach to achieving this goal in a short outline of 'culturised planning'. Prior to this discussion, however, I briefly survey the nature, operation and conceptualisation of culture in the twentieth century and for the contemporary period. I focus this account by introducing and illustrating the three themes of postmodern, minority and post-industrial culture and these in turn segue into a discussion of contemporary culturisation. Culturisation and culturised planning are accompanied with detailed tables to illustrate the strength and nature of this globalised cultural and planning innovation.

Culture's voice

In spite of the fact that culture is embedded in geographies, societies and histories, its voice in planning is feeble, and all too often tokenistic, brittle and favouring a narrow social base. There are perhaps two main reasons for culture's low profile and imbalance. First, the power of culture as an organising concept has only lately begun to be perceived, or utilised in planning, and second, there remains too great a focus in planning systems and practices on technical and mechanical issues often inherited from planning modernism. Of course, this is not to say that culture has not for some time been included in specific planning sectors, but rather that this inclusion has been mainly carried out in an opportunistic fashion. By this I mean that cultural elements, interpretation and understanding have been utilised in a piecemeal fashion that aims to cherrypick such resources. Plentiful examples of this practice abound, in particular in the urban development and redevelopment sector, where heritage buildings, relics and motifs, as well as historical images, periods and themes, are often incorporated in a de-contextualised fashion as commercial lures. Nevertheless, this kind of inclusion reflects quite directly a worldwide pattern in which cultural production is, as Allen Scott writes in *The Cultural Economy of Cities* (2000), 'increasingly commodified while commodities themselves are increasingly invested with symbolic value'. This is clearly represented in the growth of the cultural economy especially, for example, in the fields of advertising, marketing, the arts and the media. And, as Graeme Evans notes in *Cultural Planning: An Urban Renaissance?* (2001), the arts do not escape the trend as they can be commodified as urban cultural assets.

Needless to say, in contrast to these trends there are countervailing forces at work often centred on the community arena, the activities of social enterprises, the humanistic policy recommendations of the international state and non-government organisations (NGOs) and innovations such as cultural mapping and culturisation. Community cultural mapping as developed in the Australian form in 1995, and culturised planning as an evolving trend in global planning, both aim to promote more sensitive and ethical planning. The goal they share is to enable culture to speak more fully and on its own terms.

Culture today

The voice of culture has nowadays acquired unprecedented authority and interest in society and this is spilling into planning. Culture's role as a new fulcrum for societies, economies and environments presents a remarkable opportunity for planning. This position is widely advocated by United Nations agencies, advisers to these bodies such as the World Commission on Culture and Development (WCC) and numerous important theorists and commentators who argue the indispensable value of cultural integration. Among others, these include the geographer Manuel Castells (1998), the planning theorist Leonie Sandercock (2003) and the urbanist Charles Landry (2000). What this collective global experience suggests is that the well-documented 'cultural turn' of the late twentieth century, as described by David Chaney (1994), implies new and far-reaching possibilities for the sensitive uptake of culture in contemporary planning and governance, building on conceptual progress in the understanding of culture over the last century.

At the same time as the growth in understanding occurs, planning practices and planning systems themselves are being slowly transformed. To take but one example, planning is recognising and responding to the growth and importance of cultural diversity, and this affords a new relevance to planning, apparent in the areas of social planning and planning for heritage and tourism. It also impacts the design and development sectors, and in sustainability approaches, as reflected in the cultural perspective of the Agenda 21 of the United Nations 'Rio Summit' and the more recent Agenda 21 for Culture of the United Cities and Local Governments organisation (UCLG).

Culture and planning in the twentieth century

In the United Kingdom and Australasia prior to World War II, and in particular up until the watershed period of the 1970s, the dominant concept of culture was that of high culture. This elitist conception was most famously defined in the late nineteenth century by Matthew Arnold, as 'the best which has been thought and said in the world'. With the onset of the 1960s and 1970s, a rival concept of culture gained traction, based on culture as 'a whole way of life' as defined by Raymond Williams in his *Culture and Society 1780–1950*, first published in 1958. This emergent concept influenced society and planning increasingly and is now dominant. However, throughout this period the rival concepts of culture reflected distinctive cultural and social bases and interests, although they were differentially integrated into planning with little awareness of contradiction. The idea of high culture, for example, was uppermost in planning's 'mainstream' land-based activities, namely the statutory and spatial sectors of planning with a close nexus to power and capital. More up-to-date ideas about culture were influential on planning's perceived margins of social and cultural planning, as I argue in *Planning History* (vol. 27, 2005).

Raymond Williams' concept of culture as a way of life (along with the nineteenth-century anthropological concept of culture) emphasised the need to interpret cultural variation and this encouraged the culture and values that inhered in working-class lives, in indigenous cultures and in residual centres to be taken into consideration and valued as important. The concept of culture as a whole way of life was plural and necessarily implied minorities as represented, for example, by subcultures and migrant, ethnic and gay and lesbian communities.

At the global level, in spite of the cynicism of many commentators, the United Nations' efforts in conceptualising and creating standards for many aspects of culture were also useful in defining opportunities for planning. Added to this, developing views from the late twentieth century grew to emphasise both the foundational nature of culture for all development and planning as well as the manner in which contemporary culture operates and expands through itself in a postmodern age.

Culture and global policy
Woven into the preceding history of the understanding of culture in the period since World War II are the important layers of UNESCO philosophy and documents on culture, its forms, social priorities and uses. The founding document of the United Nations (UN), the *Universal Declaration of Human Rights* (1948), occupied a key, catalytic role as it identified cultural rights as rights that define humanity. The concept of sustainability was integrated into planning at the Rio Summit and its Agenda 21 nominated local cultural awareness as the foundation for the practical implementation of sustainability strategies for cultures and their environments. In the 1990s a number of the strands of earlier thinking coalesced in the findings of UNESCO's key adviser on culture, the WCC in its report, *Our Creative Diversity* (1995) which argued that cultural policy should not only be profoundly sensitive to culture but should also be inspired by it. Later in 2004, the UCLG, the peak international body for local governments, released its Agenda 21 for Culture, adding culture to the social, economic and environmental categories as the so-called fourth pillar of sustainability following the work of Jon Hawkes. Since then, the UCLG has been prominent in promoting the inclusion of this approach in the UN's new Millennium Development Goals scheduled for 2015. In these ways then, and in a clearly

self-conscious sense, our age has begun to define itself in cultural terms, making the location, articulation and integration of culture in social technologies a paramount contemporary concern.

Cultural mapping

In addition to expanding concepts of heritage, a landmark project was undertaken by the Australian Government in 1995 to develop an ethical methodology for community cultural mapping to be related to all dimensions of culture, including its tangible and intangible elements. The consultancy, which I undertook jointly with the Australian Institute of Aboriginal and Torres Strait Islander Studies (AIATSIS), published the guide *Mapping Culture: A Guide for Cultural and Economic Development in Communities* (1995). The guide describes cultural mapping in the following way:

> Cultural mapping involves a community identifying and documenting local cultural resources. Through this research cultural elements are recorded – the tangibles like galleries, craft industries, distinctive landmarks, local events and industries, as well as the intangibles like memories, personal histories, attitudes and values. After researching the elements that make a community unique, cultural mapping involves initiating a range of community activities or projects, to record, conserve and use these elements... the most fundamental goal of cultural mapping is to help communities recognise, celebrate, and support cultural diversity for economic, social and regional development.

The guide was designed to help articulate cultural diversity and values through exploring culture in a comprehensive fashion. The technique sought to encourage the social sharing and exchange of culture and values – through the sharing of food, stories, histories and places (for more, see my article, 'Cultural Mapping: Capturing Social Value, Challenging Silence', 1994). Revealing the diversity of cultural values and associations and creating new readings and meanings is something to be achieved in partnership with communities, specialists, and custodians of knowledge. The methodology drew on the development of Indigenous cultural rights in Australia, including land rights, which had strengthened considerations of attachments to land and their social value across Australia. (In 1992 the High Court of Australia in its *Mabo* decision recognised native title to land). This period in Australian history also illustrates the importance of non-mainstream cultures in influencing dominant cultural concepts, especially in the area of variations in cultural meaning.

The expansion of culture: The expansion of planning

As foreshadowed at the beginning of this chapter, I will introduce three themes to focus this account by illustrating the context of the expansion of planning and culture, mainly in Australian terms. The three themes encompass the postmodern world and its search for social communication and meaning; the ubiquity of minority cultures; and the qualities of the new post-industrial age. Each theme has a particular planning reality that can be separated out quite clearly. For example, postmodern theory in Australia has provided new categories and themes which can be empolyed in strategic planning for marketing, tourism and interpretation, and new phenomenological and hermeneutic tools sensitive enough to capture important community values. These latter tools have been introduced, for example, in the research of migrant culture and the spaces of home. Planning for Indigenous culture in the postcolonial context of Australia has also achieved some notable innovations especially in relation to understanding the importance of variations in cultural meaning. Again, in post-industrial planning for cityports such as Sydney, planners have sought to integrate regional and local culture in sustainable, regional renewal strategies encompassing elements such as ways of life, history, traditions, heritage and cultural meanings.

Postmodern culture

Postmodern social and cultural theories emphasise the rise and importance of values, difference and diversity in cultures. In an era identified in this way, planning has a critical role in recognising and responding to the diversity of all ways of life as they evolve and are expressed. The role of cultural interpretation emerges in this context as primary, and the planner becomes a facilitator in the process with communities. The research and recording of culture has become a means for communities and stakeholders to give voice to inclusive aspects of culture that might otherwise remain outside the picture. Cultural mapping, as developed in the earlier cited guide *Mapping Culture,* is a structured technique positioned to capitalise on the whole culture of a place and to give voice to cultures and communities that are facing neglect or marginalisation whether in urban and regional terms or in the context of policy and research. It also has a simpler dimension, as for example in an early Cultural Map of the Australian Capital Territory (ACT), developed using elements of the flexible cultural mapping methodology. A 'top-down' map was prepared by the ACT Government as a website with an information and tourism role to permit viewers' insights into the ACT through the use of click-on categories for the Territory's history, Aboriginal culture, multiculturalism, places, people, events and tours.

Minority culture

In a postcolonial world overlain by a North-South divide, the movement of people and the growth of migrant communities in large urban centres pose specific challenges for planning in terms of its response to diversity and the promotion of equality and harmony. Planning of this kind will be based on understanding and accommodating difference. Minorities possess a shared history of difference and often a burden of disadvantage that may be addressed in culturally specific terms through policy and planning. Migration is a common and enduring global thread for many cities. For example, Sydney, New South Wales (NSW), has experienced waves of migration from Europe and Asia in the decades since World War II, and the communities based on this migration have redefined society under official policies of multiculturalism and cultural diversity. Gay and lesbian communities have also grown in strength and diversity in Sydney and kindred cities, and so-called 'pink' planning for Sydney's Oxford Street, Darlinghurst, which encompasses the route of the annual Sydney Gay and Lesbian Mardi Gras, has minimised gay and lesbian harassment and vilification.

At every level, planning with culture may be closely involved in strengthening communities and in encouraging broader recognition and acceptance of diversity, whether reflected in different social needs, varied concepts of heritage and community places, or of the nature and importance of domestic family space. To do this successfully, planning must rely on up-to-date concepts of culture and techniques such as cultural mapping if it is to 'read' the community in sensitive and subtle terms and to engage it as a partner. The gastronomy, music, writing, religion and politics of

Figure 1. Sydney 'surfboards' satirising the city's iconography and beach culture, Sydney's Gay and Lesbian Mardi Gras, Australia (Photo: Garrie Maguire).

these communities are all cultural references that assist the planner in the work of interpretation. In this sense, culture is the basis of understanding difference.

In Australia, Indigenous communities have embraced cultural research including cultural mapping. Projects include the mapping of attachments to rural land or 'country' and urban places, the history of families and sustainable environmental and ecological practices. Bi-cultural history has emerged and is the basis of bi-cultural strategic planning for cultural heritage places, which integrate different cultural knowledges and techniques in a shared vision. This is a vision that draws on local cultural knowledge, respects custodianship and traditional Indigenous law and presents the planning framework in terms and language accessible to all sides.

Post-industrial culture
Culture is now being strongly engaged at the strategic level in regional planning in developed countries, especially in promoting the claims of major cities as centres for investment and visitation. On another level, culture is also being promoted by the WCC and the World Bank as an integral part of any development project or program in the developing world. These two approaches have culture in common and both mobilise culture as the key to environmental sustainability and social and economic success. For example, with the decline of waterfront areas in cityports globally in the 1980s, culture came to be successfully mobilised in a number of these cities as the basis for reinvention strategies designed to highlight regional differentiation and to satisfy the authenticity demanded by local communities. In Barcelona, Spain, a combination of museums devoted to the urban, artistic, maritime and political history of the city and refurbished waterfront areas and promenades and attractions together built on the city's cultural strengths and improved its image. The effect was a practical and perceptual renaissance. In Venice, Italy, the city's historic Arsenale, neglected for most of the twentieth century,

was revitalised as a high-tech centre for marine research and the development of technologies for environmental repair, along with major conference facilities. In Sydney, NSW, the significant heritage of harbour islands relating to convictism, shipbuilding and naval industries was in a number of cases conserved and adapted with new, compatible uses. At the famous Cockatoo Island with its convict buildings and historic dry-docks, these uses include filmmaking and entertainment, such as the Cockatoo Island Festival. This approach built on an earlier strategic planning vision that emphasised the Indigenous and multicultural history of Sydney Harbour and its role as a migration gateway, as I indicate in the article 'Behind the Venetians' (2000) and in Chapter 9 of *Reshaping Planning with Culture* (2008).

Figure 2. A harbour island's heritage of naval and maritime industry, Cockatoo Island (from the air), Sydney Harbour, Australia (Photo: Sydney Harbour Federation Trust).

Figure 3. A community festival celebrating an urban heartland, Cockatoo Island Festival, Sydney Harbour, Australia, 2005 (Photo: Sydney Harbour Federation Trust).

Barcelona, Venice and Sydney have all taken their place in a post-industrial world that thrives on culture as a source of productivity and wealth. In this way, the cultural strengths of cities and regions can promote urban creativity and ultimately a successful image for attracting visitors, mobile capital and symbolic workers. Peter Hall in *Cities in Civilization* (1998) describes this process and its results in the following way:

> Rich, affluent, cultivated nations and cities sell their virtue, beauty, philosophy, their art and their theatre to the rest of the world. From a manufacturing economy we pass to an informational economy, and from an informational economy to a cultural economy.

A critical aspect of the passage Hall describes is that all life and all culture have become increasingly self-referential, and it is to the implications of this and the new techniques of culturised planning that I now turn.

Culturisation and culturised planning

The absence of a workable, general model and suitable concepts and language to describe and promote the integration of culture in planning has been apparent to deeper practitioners and theorists internationally for a period of decades. My own response to this need was to research and develop a cultural model and concept to promote and give traction to the integration of culture in planning. For this purpose, I coined the term 'culturisation' in the article 'The Culturisation of Planning', published in *Planning Theory* in 2008. The model and concept were intended to facilitate culture's incorporation in planning and to introduce culture as the foundation of planning. My proposal for culturisation also identified the value of a systematic research process that was ethical, critical and reflexive. It showed the way forward for integrating both contemporary and historical cultural knowledge, along with a plurality of theory and imaginative interpretation in all spatial and strategic planning. At the time, I also flagged the value and potential application of the term to the culturisation of governance across multiple sectors and to other social technologies in addition to planning. In the same year, a full and detailed model for culturised planning was provided in the book *Reshaping Planning with Culture* (2008). In 2013 this was followed by a proposal for a cultural paradigm for planning and governance in the chapter 'Stealing the Fire of Life' in *The Ashgate Research Companion to Planning and Culture*. In this chapter I argue that culture is the true basis of planning, as it is possible to view culture as both the object of planning and as its principal 'operative' means.

The Culturised Model for Planning

I will give a brief outline of the Culturised Model for Planning to indicate its value and potential application and to indicate the relevance of community cultural mapping as a culturised practice. The full model is contained in *Reshaping Planning with*

Culture where it is illustrated with examples from around the globe and in two detailed Australian case studies. In the first case study, spatial planning is outlined in relation to culture at every planning scale for Sydney, from the metropolitan scale down to a single allotment of land in the historic inner suburb of Ultimo. The second case study utilises a World Heritage Site, the Port Arthur Historic Site, Tasmania, to illustrate the model in respect of non-spatial strategic planning and to show that it is in principle applicable to any protected area globally. The understanding behind the model grew cumulatively out of my original work as a historian and environmental advocate in Australia and was furthered by developing the Australian model for cultural mapping in the mid-1990s and subsequent global academic research and planning practice.

The model consists of three elements: 1) Seven Principles for Culture; 2) a Planner's Literacy Trio; and 3) a Research Method based on the key concepts of holistic culture and holistic research. The model is illustrated in Table 1.

Table 1. The Culturised Model for Planning and Governance

Seven Principles for Culture	Planner's Literacy Trio	Research Method
Plenitude	Cultural,	*Holistic Culture*
Connectivity	Ethical and	*(Coherent)* –
Diversity	Strategic Literacy	Society, History and
Reflexivity		Environment
Creativity		
Critical Thinking		*Holistic Research*
Sustainability		*(Integrated)* –
		Cultural Data Research
		Cultural Collaborations
		Cultural Interpretation

Source: Greg Young, 2012

126

Seven Principles for Culture, The Planner's Literacy Trio and the Culturised Research Methodology

The role of the Seven Principles for Culture in the model is to support and provide context for the work of the research method, but they also may be used in their own right as educational and community tools. The origin, purpose and applications of the principles are fully illustrated in *Reshaping Planning with Culture*. The trio of cultural, ethical and strategic literacies interlock with the Seven Principles for Culture. The Culturised Research Methodology includes two elements, a concept of holistic culture and a concept of holistic research. The concept of holistic culture divides the slippery world of culture into useable categories comprising society, history and the environment as well as the tangible and intangible forms of culture and culture's historical and contemporary manifestations. In this way, culture and its constituents are made 'legible' for planning and broader governance purposes. The three dimensions of culture are illustrated in Table 2 as they are reflected in philosophical concepts, key disciplines and everyday language.

Table 2. Holistic Culture in three dimensions in Philosophy, Key Disciplines and Everyday Language

Philosophy	Key Disciplines	Everyday Language
Space	Geography	Environment
Time	History	Heritage
Society	Sociology	Society/ways-of-life

Source: Greg Young, 2013

Working in tandem with the power of holistic culture is the more comprehensive access to culture offered through the practice of holistic research. Holistic research practices are required to address contemporary cultural and social diversity, current levels of planning complexity and the continuous social need to interpret culture. Holistic research provides a method to 'scan' the research world for all materials that are potentially relevant to make them available to planning as well as for use in cultural mapping projects. Holistic research consists of three interpenetrated elements: cultural data research, cultural collaboration and cultural interpretation.

Cultural data research is best described as quantitative research and is based on information derived from sources such as census statistics, public records, historical records and environmental data. This information is usually in the public domain and is often available online in the form of databases, digitised archives, encyclopedias and global literatures. Collaborative cultural research is sourced from more communicative processes that involve community engagement and participation in numerous areas of the plan–making process, using techniques such as action research, cultural mapping, community histories and a broad range of community projects. Cultural interpretation, for its part, values and utilises the insights and knowledge located through and in cultural theory, the social sciences, political economy, academic and popular history, the humanities, the arts and indigenous understanding and values. Although not an exhaustive list, holistic research is illustrated in sample form in Table 3.

The Culturised Research Methodology is a holistic innovation because each pathway to culture is considered potentially relevant to planning in some way. Combined with a holistic view of culture, the qualities of each dimension of culture may be animated in order to flow through all aspects of the planning process so that 'no stone is left unturned'. Figure 4 illustrates the Culturised Research Methodology and its interrelated components in a sequential fashion in order to suggest the dynamics of a culturised research process in one image.

Table 3. Holistic Research

Cultural Data Research	Cultural Collaboration	Cultural Interpretation
Online data	Online collaborations	Interpretation/s online
Social media, blogs	Wikis, bulletin boards	
Census data	Consultations	Behavioural, psychological and communication theories
Project Gutenberg	Story-telling in different modes	
Historical records		Structuralist theories
	Action research	
Environmental data		Postmodern social and cultural theory/ studies
	Cultural mapping	
Cultural mapping		
	In-depth interviews	
Heritage places		Cultural mapping
	Oral histories, community histories and memories	
Cultural infrastructure		Storytelling, discourse analysis and semiotics
Arts and humanities		
	Community projects e.g. gardens, the arts and sustainability	
Music, fiction, poetry		Indigenous understanding
Religion		Academic history
Emergent culture		Feminism and queer theory

Source: Greg Young, 2012

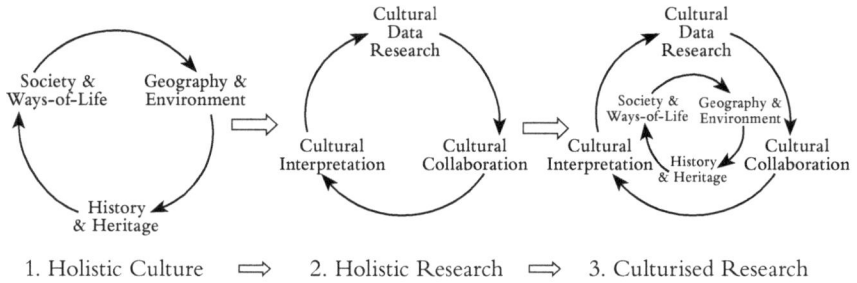

Figure 4. The Culturised Research Methodology for Planning and Governance

Conclusion

For culture to speak like Vladimir Nabokov's powerful and all-engaging memory it will need to be present and realised in all planning in a critical, ethical and reflective sense. The preceding perspective of culturisation and the culturised model are designed to promote this opportunity utilising holistic culture and holistic research, and these approaches are increasingly influential in international academic research and planning practice. Over time, they should further assist in the better synthesis of culture in planning, as well as serve to promote richer and more humane and sustainable relationships between planning, society and the environment. Owing to the fact that culturisation is based on whole culture and the possibilities of a plurality of theory, it has the capability to draw in culture through a multiplicity of conceptual and methodological approaches that include cultural mapping. A holistic view of culture may also supplant the often narrow, selective and non-inclusive concepts of culture that lead to blinkered planning. Cultural mapping for example is able to work across different epistemologies and to encourage cross-fertilisation between diverse theoretical and interpretive insights. In overall terms, culturisation variously supports cultural approaches such as culturised planning, community cultural mapping and the introduction of stronger cultural positioning to policies such as the global Millennium Development Goals. As a way forward, such approaches may be fostered through innovative collaborations and exchanges between all partners and levels, such as local communities, cultural workers, planning practitioners, state and local governments and the international state and NGOs. In this fashion, and over time, culture in policy and planning may be empowered to speak more fully of itself and in critical, ethical and reflective terms.

CASE STUDIES

Young and Savvy:
Indigenous Hip-hop
as Regional Cultural Asset

Andrew Warren and Rob Evitt

This chapter explores how Indigenous youth from two socio-economically disadvantaged places – one in Australia's tropical north, the other just beyond the outermost edge of the Greater Sydney metropolitan area – marshal resources and find expressive voice through hip-hop music, dance and video production. In these locations, physical distance and poverty are conditions influencing the ability of creative artists to do their work, access opportunities and build careers. Yet remoteness is managed, and marginality negotiated through the expressive medium of hip-hop and new recording and distribution technologies. Through their efforts, Indigenous hip-hoppers have built a new kind of network – semi-informal, political, transnational and often decidedly anti-colonial – that constitutes a new, vernacular, Indigenous creative industry in regional and remote Australia.

But crucially, we also explore how physical distance and poverty are not the only barriers that creative artists negotiate. Young musicians navigate expectations of themselves and what constitutes 'proper' Indigenous performance in wider Australian cultural industries. Beyond physical and socio-economic margin-ality, cultural norms and expectations frame what are possible, producing and restricting creative opportunities.

The chapter draws on collaboration from 2008 to 2009 between two researchers – one Indigenous, one non-Indigenous (both having grown up in the Southern Illawarra) – who brought to this project different goals and backgrounds. Andrew was at the time a PhD researcher on the Cultural Asset Mapping in Regional Australia (CAMRA) project. Rob is Indigenous and belongs to the Yirandali Aboriginal nation, in the Hughenden area of north-west Queensland. At the time of research he was a student and active member of the region's Indigenous hip-hop scene. This collaboration provided unique links and personal connections that fostered fieldwork.

Indigenous culture and cultural assets

Within cultural policy and planning, Indigenous culture has often been assumed as static rather than a culture always in creation, and to belong to a singular, homogenous community rather than one in which there are traditional and contemporary, nostalgic and dissident voices. Dominant stereotypes – like those mobilised in tourism and cultural industry promotion, especially visual art – have presumed that Indigenous culture is bounded by tradition, ethnicity and heritage. Instead, Marcia Langton in her highly influential 1993 essay 'Well, I Heard It on the Radio and I Saw It on the Television' (written originally for the Australian Film Commission) argued that Indigenous identity was much more inter-subjective, 'in that it is re-made over and over in a process of dialogue, imagination, representation and interpretation'. Media forms including television, film, literature and music are important avenues for understanding how Aboriginal concerns and voices are imagined, represented and interpreted.

In regional Australia, the question is also arbitrated by geography and industry. Place is crucial; sites of creation and birth, ceremony, celebration, historical and spiritual, places of loss, memory and grief. At another level, industries that sell Indigenous creativity frequently trade on images and designs that market Aboriginal culture. This has profound implications for emerging Indigenous cultural industries and their success (or otherwise) in markets beyond Indigenous audiences. Typically, dot or x-ray art painted by artists from remote communities, or music containing didjeridu (*yidaki* in Yolngu) is considered 'proper' Aboriginal creativity and promoted to tourists and visitors to northern Australia. Meanwhile, more contemporary or avant-garde activities escape touristic and commercial representation.

Against this backdrop, what has emerged across regional, rural and urban Aboriginal Australia is a lively, fluid and challenging hip-hop scene that transgresses boundaries between art and popular culture, 'local' and 'global', legal and illegal, informal subculture and legitimate 'industry'. We pursued interviews with Indigenous hip-hoppers in two very different places – Nowra in New South Wales, and in the Torres Strait Islands – asking questions about how they negotiate physical remoteness and displacement, as well as expectations of their creativity.

Hip-hop: A transnational language of black culture and politics

Originating as a music format in the disadvantaged urban neighbourhoods of the Bronx, Harlem and Brooklyn in New York during the 1970s, and further building on Jamaican sound system culture, hip-hop traditionally involves dee-jaying (beat), rapping (MC), breakdancing (B-boying) and graffiti elements. Its commercialisation has steadily transformed the genre from an underground element of urban culture to a mainstream, global industry, with its own distinct language, embracing fashion brands FUBU and Tommy Hilfiger. Aspiring young rappers have begun replacing dee-jaying elements with music software allowing at-home creation, cutting together different instruments to form unique instrumental sounds or beats.

Locality and authenticity are vital to hip-hop. For many black American youth in the 1980s and 1990s, disenfranchised with life in urban ghettos, hip-hop enabled articulation of oral stories confronting daily life on the streets: gang-related violence, extortion and drug dealing. To traverse, navigate and make sense of daily struggles, youth turned to hip-hop. Many listened and danced to rappers and DJs playing on street corners, before trying hip-hop. As underground and oppositional, street-performed hip-hop grew increasingly popular in cities across the United States, drawing large crowds for neighbourhood 'bloc parties'.

By the late 1990s, hip-hop was the highest-selling musical genre in America. Commercial, yet still confrontational and oppositional, hip-hop was globalised via CD, television and fashion, becoming a vehicle of expression and identification, particularly relevant for working-class, migrant and Indigenous youth. Disenfranchised groups related to the identities and circumstances behind the music; it was linguistically powerful, at times arrogant – a platform where minority bodies and voices were thrust into elevated positions in the media landscape (especially in music video clips).

In Australia hip-hop became popular amongst Indigenous youth, where influence from American hip-hoppers Ice Cube, TuPac Shakur, Snoop Dogg and Jay Z was strong. The uptake of hip-hop by Indigenous Australia can also be attributed to an evolving 'transnational black culture'. While hip-hop is a global language, positioned around ideas of brotherhood and resistance, it is also an open soundtrack for interpretation and 'flushing' by local experiences, appealing to young Aboriginal people asserting Indigenous identity while valorising global black experiences.

When performing in Australia, artists like Snoop Dogg and Ice Cube have made efforts to connect with local Aboriginal populations, referring to cultural similarities during interviews and gigs, as well as by making physical contact with communities, as Snoop Dogg has done, in Sydney's Redfern. A number of local performers have also played a significant role in indigenising hip-hop in Australia, actively tutoring and mentoring emerging and grassroots enthusiasts, hosting workshops, teaching skills and providing direct musical support. Aboriginal performers MC Munki Mark, Wire MC and Brothablack provide cultural and creative learning for budding indigenous artists. Their music advocates pride and solidarity, projecting Indigeneity as brotherhood. These pedagogies help develop slick rhyming and language, performance and self-confidence through rapping.

Not restricted to Sydney, Melbourne or Brisbane, Indigenous musicians are practicing and performing hip-hop in remote and isolated communities in places like Wilcannia (Wilcannia Mob), Bowraville (Bowra Rhythm Mob) and Kununurra (G-Unit). These locations have nascent hip-hop scenes despite geographical distance from Australia's traditional music industry centres. In these places, hip-hop becomes a form of cultural expression, a means to personal development, and simultaneously a politicised, transnational and anti–colonial creative industry.

Research contexts: Nowra and the Torres Strait Islands

Nowra, the main town in the Shoalhaven Local Government Area on the south coast of New South Wales, has a resident population of 30,000. During summer holidays the town bulges as tourists pass through to access holiday spots in nearby Jervis Bay, Sussex Inlet and Ulladulla. Yet seasonal tourist traffic has brought Nowra limited economic or social benefit. Being inland, Nowra's share in the tourism boom has been limited, instead constituting a regional service and retail centre along the major highway. It is a place characterised by high youth unemployment levels, out-migration and welfare dependence. According to the national population census, some 6 per cent of the population identify as Indigenous, a high proportion compared with national and state figures (2.1 per cent and 2.3 per cent, respectively), with one in five Indigenous people in Nowra aged 15 to 24. In formal education, only 16 per cent of Aboriginal youth complete a year 12 education in Nowra, compared to 31 per cent for non-Indigenous youth (and contrasted to the national average of 42 per cent). Unemployment amongst the Indigenous population is 22 per cent, with a third of Indigenous youth aged 15 to 24 unemployed.

Positioned at the margins of economic growth and social life, Nowra is a town facing complex problems, retaining a reputation for racial tensions, high rates of crime and violence, particularly in East Nowra, where around 20 per cent of the population is Indigenous. Stigmas are commonly attached to Indigenous youth in the town, depicted as delinquent, idle and troublesome. This is the background for hip-hop in Nowra as vernacular Indigenous creativity.

The Torres Strait Islands, meanwhile, located off the coast of far north Queensland, could hardly be more different to Nowra. The Islands are home to 9,000 residents scattered across 17 inhabited tropical islands. More than 80 per cent of the population in the Torres Strait Islands identifies as Indigenous, related ethnically to Melanesia further to the north rather than to mainland Aboriginal nations. The dominant spoken languages are Torres Strait Islands Creole and other traditional Island dialects. Overall, the Torres Strait Islands comprise around 11 per cent of Australia's Indigenous population, but only 14 per cent of Indigenous Islanders still live in the Islands. The physical distance of the Torres Strait Islands from the 'rest' of Australia cannot be easily overstated. Thursday Island, the main population centre, is more than 3,500 km from Melbourne and 2,000 km from Brisbane. Limited links exist with the mainland, commonly with Cairns (because of air transport), in far north Queensland. Remoteness is a tangible part of everyday life.

Although contrasting wildly in cultural and geographical terms, socio-economic trends in the Torres Strait Islands share some similarities with Nowra. Again, according to the national population census, the Indigenous population is four times more likely to be unemployed and more than twice as likely to be living in a low-income household compared to the non-Indigenous Torres Strait Islands population. Moreover, the retention rate in formal education for Indigenous youth in the Islands is half that of non-Indigenous youth; a similar ratio holds for non-school qualifications, such as a trade or diploma.

In these two socio-economically disadvantaged and geographically marginal settings, flourishing Indigenous hip-hop scenes have emerged, overwhelmingly dominated by young people. Here hip-hop is an example of creativity inspired by transnational cultural flows (and attendant linguistic and political features), but forming and operating within local spaces, geographically removed and socio-economically isolated from prosperous cities.

Methods and tools: Researching Indigenous hip-hop

As with many of the other projects featured in this book, our research approach sought depth of insights, but needed to remain flexible. The project initially focused on Nowra, concerned with 'hanging out' and meeting young people involved in music. The local youth centre became a key research location, regularly utilised by youth participating in hip-hop. Hanging out at the centre helped build friendships and trust with a number of young hip-hoppers. After initial meetings, participant observation and a research diary were used to reflect on meetings, both in situ and out of context. These notes then formed the basis for subsequent semi-structured interviews. Six young rappers were interviewed, but here we focus especially on the music produced by one hip-hop group who call themselves Yuin Soldiers, and in particular their three rappers Yung Nooky, Nat and Selway. Combining interviews and participant observation with the group's music-making provided a rich and extensive outline of processes for creating Yuin Soldiers' beats, lyrics and performances.

Next, the research drew on personal networks, expanding the focus to incorporate hip-hop from the Torres Strait Islands. Knowledge of the growing 'scene' in remote northern Australia allowed researchers to access a hip-hop crew called One Blood Hidden Image. The group consists of six members from across the Torres Straits Islands. Our interviews and subsequent conversations were conducted with four members of the group: Mau Power, Mondae, Cagney and Big Worm.

For each study location, methodologies were embraced differently. For Nowra, time could be spent moving through the youth centre, observing interactions and performances taking place within its spaces. A more ethnographic, in-depth analysis could therefore be undertaken, with data collection drawn from extended visits with participants. For the Torres Straits Islands, methodologies needed to be more flexible. It was not possible to visit islands directly; instead, in-depth phone conversations, interviews and emailing with our participants took priority.

Analysis of interviews, research notes and music then drew on an adapted form of narrative analysis. Narrative analysis focuses on how people talk about and evaluate places, experiences and situations – including, in our case, via the music itself. Our point is that these narratives – stories of place and even disputations of the status quo – are important regional cultural assets.

Producing Indigenous hip-hop

Hip-hop music has become very popular among Indigenous youth in the Torres Strait Islands, attracted to its fast, funky beats, expression and accessibility. Big Worm, the newest One Blood Hidden Image member, explained its popularity:

> We were doing it on the streets, around the Straits, fucking around, then Patrick came out with that single 'Home boys', that's when we all got like, yeah we can all do that too, you know. That's when

we started getting into it, we loved it bro. It's poetry, like what you go through [in life], it's a good opportunity to use that in hip-hop. Now we be walking around town and stuff, and these younger fellas start coming up everywhere rapping, and we like, yeah you're good man, keep it up.

One Blood Hidden Image have gained increasing exposure within the Indigenous hip-hop scene. Comprised originally of five main MCs – Patrick aka Mau Power, Josh aka Cagney, Damien aka Mondae, Dayne aka Dayne-Jah, and Leroy aka Artu, the group have since incorporated several other members, including Troy aka Big Worm. One Blood Hidden Image work to create a distinctive hip-hop sound, mixing traditional Creole language with cultural stories and messages. The music has appealed to Indigenous elders across the Torres Strait Islands, who recognise its widespread appeal for youth. According to Mau Power:

> It's Torres Strait Island hip-hop, an Indigenous hip-hop, we incorporate our language and culture into that style, that genre… We get a great response from the elders cause that's a new genre for them. They're not used to hip-hop, and we show that we can incorporate our culture into hip-hop, and they're like, WOW, keep it up.

To create and produce their own unique beats, sounds and rhymes, One Blood Hidden Image have become skilled at using computer music programs such as FruityLoops, ACID and Reason, which give aspiring hip-hoppers in remote locations the ability to sample and fuse together sounds to compose original beats, without relying on city recording studios. As Mau Power explains:

> Well I started using FruityLoops, now we have upgraded. I'm using Adobe Edition, a bit of Reason, ACID. I use Reason for the samples but I still record [raps] in Adobe.

While all performers in the group create their own beats using computer programs, Mondae is the 'lead beat master':

> I listen to the music; focus on the beats. It comes natural. Some days I can do three beats. I use the laptop and FruityLoops, go through every instrument [in the program], mix in different instruments, change up the pace, go through, clean it up, til you've got something ya like.

Making beats is a technical skill, requiring practice and refinement. Computer programs are cheaper than DJ equipment and can be self-learnt, allowing participants to sample instrumental segments from other genres. One Blood Hidden Image likes to 'cut' in reggae sounds, snare drums, with deep bass guitars, manoeuvring the pace of beats, slowing down or speeding up, depending on message and the type of song. After the beat and raps are brought together, the group records their music using Mau Power's homemade studio. Emerging technologies of hip-hop production create a more accessible, do-it-yourself (DIY) musical form.

One Blood Hidden Image's music has been uploaded onto video networking sites, especially YouTube, where tracks such as 'Coolies' and 'My Blood My People' have received between 20,000 and 50,000 hits, significant numbers for an underground, unsigned group. The band also sells and promotes their music (four albums) online via Facebook and their website, along with clothing and other merchandise (see https://soundcloud.com/maupower).

Their sound is driven and produced by modern technologies and techniques, mostly circulated electronically. Group members are often stopped in the street and praised for their music, and Mau Power was nominated for a 2009 Deadly Award (the national Indigenous music awards). Through beat-mixing, rhyming, performance, dancing and computer skills, hip-hop is a means to be creative in a remote geographic location far from the genre's urban origins.

Meanwhile, in Nowra, seemingly unassuming community infrastructure has provided space for a vibrant youth production scene. On most afternoons the Nowra Youth Centre's music rooms are occupied by groups of young hip-hoppers. Emerging here is the group Yuin Soldiers, who have a shifting line-up including Corey aka Yung Nooky, Nat and Selway, Nooky's cousin. Recognising a growing interest in hip-hop by young people from the area, the youth centre has built two music rooms for use by budding musicians for learning, practice and performing. The soundproof room allows hip-hoppers to mix beats and rhymes, record their tracks and burn them onto CDs or upload as MP3s. The services at the youth centre are crucial for grassroots music making in Nowra, providing the only free space in town to use deejaying turntables, mixing, editing and recording equipment.

The production of new songs for Yuin Soldiers, like for One Blood Hidden Image, is reliant on computer programs and technologies, creating sounds and beats for the rappers. For Nooky, creating 'cool' beats is a skill that requires practice and perseverance:

> We put the beat on there first [demonstrates on the computer screen], then we rap to the beat. You do your back-up vocals and you compress it, bounce it down and it's ready for CD. Sometimes I can do it in 40 minutes, but then sometimes it can take a few hours or days to do a song. It depends. I'm always writing. When I'm at home I write, and when I'm at school.

To assist Yuin Soldiers' hip-hop, more established Indigenous artists provide encouragement, informal schooling and even direct help with composing sounds and beats. Older performers including Wire MC, Brothablack and Street Warriors were cited as inspiration for Yuin Soldiers and their music making. Wire MC and Indigenous performer Choo Choo (CuzCo) had previously collaborated with Yuin Soldiers. For Nooky, his older cousin Selway – a skilled hip-hopper from a group called East Coast

Productions (ECP) – was another prominent figure assisting in his musical production.

One Blood Hidden Image, with most members in their twenties, have been practising and refining hip-hop over several years. Yuin Soldiers – Nooky, Selway and Nat – aged in their late teens, are younger and less experienced performers. They spoke of building up skills for music making. In the same way as One Blood Hidden Image are promoting hip-hop in the Torres Strait Islands to younger, budding hip-hoppers, 'showing them the way' (Big Worm), Yuin Soldiers have drawn on the expertise and experience of more established acts like Wire MC and Choo Choo, to advance their creative skills.

Managing and navigating remoteness through music

Each member of One Blood Hidden Image was born in different parts of the Torres Strait. This has geographic significance for the group, for, as Mau Power explains, One Blood Hidden Image invented their name through their geography:

> We were singin' like nobody, we didn't have a name; just called the rap group. The original five members were sitting around and said we want to come up with a name that could be a concept that represented us as a group. We tried to find one, because each member represents one particular region. The Torres Strait is subdivided into five different regions; we have the inner islands, the near western, the central, the top western and the eastern islands, and each member came from that blood line, those regions and we were all related. So we had a blood line connection, and so we said we all one blood, with no particular image, so we all had different forms, and that's how we evolved to One Blood Hidden Image.

Rather than allow isolation and remoteness from large cities to paralyse their creativity, One Blood Hidden Image has overcome distance through hip-hop. Combining music with new technologies, especially YouTube, the Torres Strait Islands are positioned in their hip-hop as a musical hub. Subsequently the group have uncovered opportunities to travel and experience the rest of Australia, performing their music in Brisbane, Sydney, Newcastle, Melbourne, Adelaide and Auckland. Their songs project messages about brotherhood and maintaining a positive outlook.

Cagney and Mau Power explain how isolation and remoteness were managed in the Torres Strait Islands. As the established hip-hoppers in the region, the group became involved in schooling younger budding rappers, especially in their own hip-hop production, giving the 'young fellas' something positive to do against background politics of shame. As Cagney explains:

> There's a lot of mob now starting to come out. There was a lot of shame. Shame was big up here, and so for them young kids when we up on stage, we say come down here, watch us, we notice how all of a sudden they have courage to get up themselves. We do workshops too; do up a beat and each person has a line by line. Everybody got their story and in this way even the smallest voice can be heard you know.

Overcoming the 'shame' factor, performing and expressing oneself in front of audiences is an issue facing many young people in the Torres Strait Islands. Those that have taken the 'jump' forward to performing their music have gained important benefits, according to Big Worm:

> When they have a go at the workshop, rap to the beat, the young fellas go yeah, this is cool. We get them to write their raps down, then they can record and play them back. It gives them a buzz, bro, eh? Like you see it on their faces; fuck, we can do it.

Creating hip-hop is accessible for most young fans in the Torres Strait Islands because of cheap technology and available mentoring.

Mau Power takes an active role in schooling younger enthusiasts, showing them how to set up their own recording areas in the home or garage. The local library and TAFE also provide places to practise music. While remote and marginal, the Torres Strait Islands has a growing music scene with creativity funnelled into the production of beats and rhymes.

While not as geographically remote as the Torres Strait Islands, Nowra is socio-economically and, in a certain way, also geographically marginal. This marginality is openly confronted by Yung Nooky and Nat through their raps and narratives, performing both individually and as Yuin Soldiers with Selway. When asked about the origins of their group's name, Nooky explained, 'Yuin is our people, like where we come from, and soldiers, they keep fighting and never give up, so that's where the name Yuin Soldiers came from'.

Their music confronts prejudiced experience, with Nowra seen as a place perpetuating racialised ideas of Aboriginality. One of Yuin Soldiers' songs, 'Subliminal Twist', raps about the marginality experienced by Indigenous youth in Nowra:

> Blackfella on the hunt,
> Sick of being called a little black cunt,
> While I'm walking I'm thinking,
> Is this the price of education?
> Heartache, racism and discrimination?

In parallel to their sense of displacement are feelings of attachment to Nowra and the south coast, as Nooky describes:

> Well, Nowra is where we live and grew up so it's home, that's a strong feeling, like this is your place. But it's also a place that gives you the shits. You've got to get out of Nowra for a while; it can get you down, but go away, then come back and keep goin'. It is a beautiful place and that, but it can be a pretty racist place you know?

Nowra is home, yet consciously is also a place to escape. Living in Nowra is seen as a struggle or fight for Indigenous youth, metaphorically drawn out in a Yuin Soldiers rap, where Nooky cites the town (and its postcode, 2541) and makes comparison with American boxer Rubin 'Hurricane' Carter:

> South Coast Hurricane…you can call me Rubin Carter,
> Instead of a right hook, it's the rapper Yung Nook…
> The first round's already won,
> 2541 ask around I'm the man in that town,
> I'm goin big with my South coast sound.
> Ah welcome you all to the South coast flow,
> On the map we're big, that's how we roll,
> Yeah got the endless rhymes, yeah for the endless crimes.

In Nowra's Aboriginal hip-hop, local experience is integrated with a politicised transnational black culture. Music making can be drawn from daily experiences within marginal places, providing creative stimulus for rhymes and raps. Hip-hop allows negotiation of place and circumstance through confrontation and expressivity.

Performing hip-hop

While practising in the Torres Strait Islands is considered 'easy', gaining access to performance spaces outside the islands is more difficult and attributed to the region's 'remoteness' (Mondae). Gigs have been dominantly bounded within Indigenous ceremonies, events or festivals: National Sorry Day, Reconciliation events and NAIDOC celebrations. These performances provided our musicians rare travel experiences to locations across mainland Australia; hence, they were recounted very positively.

Nevertheless, Mau Power, Mondae, Big Worm and Cagney said in interviews how remoteness in the Torres Strait Islands leaves musically talented youth frustrated, unable to access opportunities to play their music to larger audiences on the mainland, or earn any significant income from their work. One Blood Hidden Image themselves rarely receive invitations to play at music festivals or gigs outside of symbolic Indigenous events.

To improve musical skills, participants spoke of 'moving to the mainland' (Big Worm) for education and opportunity. On the mainland Mau Power and Mondae had learnt more 'formal' music skills – recording, computer programming and professional networking – called upon for accessing performance opportunities. Big Worm told of needing to 'get away' from the Torres Strait Islands, recently deciding to move to Brisbane for greater opportunities. Playing gigs to non-Indigenous audiences was rare; receiving payment for their shows or funding for recording or workshops was rarer still. Members had strong aspirations to forge professional music careers, moving away from the Torres Strait Islands, at various times, to pursue those goals. However, their ambitions of becoming professional hip-hoppers were yet to materialise, in part due to the restricted avenues for paid performance.

Yuin Soldiers also commented on the limited support for musical performance in Nowra. Indigenous celebrations such as NAIDOC events supplied the majority of their hip-hop performance opportunities. In addition to Yuin Soldiers' hip-hop, Nooky and Selway are involved in traditional Aboriginal dancing. Most performances outside of Nowra privileged their traditional Aboriginal dancing over hip-hop. It was rare for any of the young rappers to play a hip-hop gig at school for a band or music day, or at non-Indigenous music festivals. Music celebrated at these events was likely to be other genres, like punk, rock, or 'traditional' Aboriginal performances, such as didjeridu playing or dancing. As Nooky explains:

> Mostly, like the NAIDOC week people ringing me up, and like [pause] yeah there's places I have performed at, like here [Nowra Youth Centre], and I'm performing here next Friday, and up at the

showground in the middle of town but you mostly get booked out for Indigenous type events.

Nooky and his cousin Selway had performed traditional Aboriginal dances for World Youth Day in Sydney, in front of a large audience, before being invited to perform a hip-hop set to this same audience, which fused traditional dancing elements with their beats and rhymes. This was a highlight, a rare opportunity to showcase their contemporary rhyming and performance skills.

Conclusion

Hip-hop is a contemporary form of Aboriginal storytelling, over-coming socio-economic marginality and remoteness through new technologies and transnational modes of black political expression. Although positioned outside dominant understandings of acceptable, commercial Indigenous culture (meaning limited paid work opportunities), Indigenous hip-hop is nevertheless a rich cultural asset for a range of urban, rural and remote communities. Indigenous hip-hop warrants being taken much more seriously in cultural planning across diverse regions of Australia: it is 'creative' because it is concerned with being artistic, resourceful and innovative, and involves technical skill, manoeuvring, recording and performing. Through appropriation of transnational black discourse, motifs and language, Indigenous hip-hop is also a fusion between the traditional (language, cultural stories, histories and dance) and contemporary (equipment, software and technologies), and inverts the urban focus of the mainstream industry. This alone is important to acknowledge in regional Australia, where there are significant Aboriginal populations. Moreover, Indigenous hip-hop enables local Aboriginal youth to perform music, express themselves and to negotiate, emotively and politically, their socio-economic circumstances.

New media and communication technologies have increased in geographic scope in the last decade and, although not evenly accessible everywhere, have become much more pervasive. Production and consumption of music is increasingly reliant on these emerging technologies. Individual songs, albums and entire discographies are downloaded from iTunes or LimeWire in minutes, transferring music to CD and MP3 players. Programs and software help develop unique sounds and beats, often replacing the need to learn musical instruments. Music can be made at home or at the local youth centre, recorded and uploaded to YouTube or Facebook sites. In turn, these networks spread music to larger audiences, promoting skills and ambitions of grassroots and underground performers, as well as signed professionals.

Indigenous hip-hop production requires a combination of underlying telecommunications infrastructure (adequate in Nowra and the Torres Strait, but still woeful in large parts of rural and remote Australia) and progressive thinking by local social workers and community planners. In the case of Nowra, the youth centre allows and encourages young people to be creative – prosaic community infrastructure enabling cultural activity of significance. Indigenous hip-hop is an evolving musical form, providing an important platform where young musicians express identities, creativity, passions and skill. The hope of the musicians featured in this chapter (and the authors) is that in the future aspiring Indigenous hip-hop artists will have improved opportunities to progress musical flair and talent into viable professional careers. Access to relevant musical equipment, infrastructure, mentoring and performance opportunities are crucial to the future development of a vibrant Indigenous hip-hop.

An earlier version of this chapter, 'Indigenous Hip-hop: Overcoming Marginality, Encountering Constraints', was published in *Australian Geographer*, vol. 41, 2010, pp. 141–58.

Engaging Creativity in Industrial Regions: Mapping Vernacular Cultural Assets

Chris Gibson, Andrew Warren and Ben Gallan

This chapter explores the vernacular cultural assets of Wollongong, a largely suburban industrial city located just to the south of Sydney. Our interest here stems from our research for the wider Cultural Asset Mapping in Regional Australia (CAMRA) project, which asked the following key questions: outside of official planning discourses, what kinds of cultural assets exist in a rapidly changing and historically industrial region? What constitutes creativity in such a context? And, as researchers, what kinds of research practice are necessary to engage with marginalised social groups and working-class communities as part of a cultural asset mapping approach? In this chapter, we reflect on our research experiences, and discuss the particularities of cultural and creative practice in a working-class steel city that is undergoing transitions. The story includes surfboards, punk music and custom-designed cars, but also diverse suburban 'cool places' invisible to the creative cities script.

At the outset, no presumptions were made about what creativity might be, where it resides in the city, or its importance to cultural planning practice. Creative industries audits had already been conducted for Wollongong, and the contours of conventional arts activities in the city were already well known. A different approach to informing cultural planning was needed. A more meaningful influence was the growing field of community-engaged research for arts and cultural planning, which emphasises processes and outcomes related to concerns with social justice and cultural diversity – the politics of knowledge production as significant as the knowledge created. Cultural asset mapping for us meant negotiating with regional research partners, navigating the politics of knowledge-generation and delivering tangible 'data' on grassroots culture and creativity, while embracing the possibility of diverse activities and perspectives without prescribing fixed methods.

The setting for our research was Wollongong, an archetypal blue-collar industrial Australian city, in the wider Illawarra region, historically dominated by the coal and steel industries and facing ongoing fears around deindustrialisation. This setting amplifies the relevance of exploring vernacular creativity and cultural assets, for it reveals the particular way regional economic futures are imagined. This case illuminates how youth and vernacular working-class cultures have tended to be forsaken within a desire to find new regional economic narratives, in places burdened with the reputation of being imperilled by global economic forces.

In Wollongong, one policy prescription has been to embrace 'creativity' as a strategy for ensuring economic futures. The dominant policy view is that cities shrug off rust-belt identities and adapt economic development strategies that foster 'creativity', diversify local economies, create jobs, attract tourists, and appeal to a creative class of in-migrants. In this view, an industrial heritage can be a burden; creative-industry promotion then becomes a means to jettison brown industrial images and infrastructure in favour of streetwise, bohemian and cosmopolitan imagery.

Nevertheless, 'creative' has tended to be articulated through conventional understandings of the arts: supporting galleries and performance centres and incubating innovation in corporate science, technology and engineering sectors. There are presences of what are typically described as 'creative industries' in Wollongong, including a theatre scene, visual artists, filmmakers and designers – and the city has pockets of gentrified 'creative class' activity, partly in the inner city and also on its scenic northern beaches (a function of lifestyle and amenity). Many gains have been made in Wollongong, but benefits have been unevenly distributed: a stark north–south socio-economic divide persists within the city; regional youth unemployment remains high; retraining schemes for workers who lost jobs in heavy industry have had mixed results; and long-term dislocation of manufacturing workers has not been sufficiently countered by growth in new industries. This was the setting within which researchers were charged with the task of mapping vernacular cultural assets – as imagined by residents themselves.

Adding to the urgency of this task was that the kinds of arts and cultural activities previously promoted often reinforced middle-class metropolitan tastes while denigrating local working-class people as somehow 'less creative' (one Wollongong suburb was infamously voted Australia's 'most bogan place' in a nationwide poll). Typical are slickly branded campaigns revolving around middle-class aesthetics and a predilection for bourgeois consumption spaces rather than enterprises that generate jobs and production. Another danger was that previously the enormous creative potential residing in economically oppressed social groups had been neglected – a question of fundamental social justice as well as cultural planning.

Wollongong City Council cultural planners, who were industry partners on the CAMRA project, wanted to include well-established arts communities in the research, but also – mindful of the critiques of creativity and class alluded to above – wished to explore a more expansive understanding of what creativity might be, and where it could be found. An open-minded approach was important in Wollongong: with its industrial base, strong working-class culture and challenging demographic mix (high levels of cultural diversity, newly arrived migrant and refugee communities, socio-economic inequality, and problems of youth unemployment), any project focusing only on the established arts and creative industries would quickly run the risk of reinforcing existing divides and appear elitist.

Negotiating methods and pragmatic research journeys

Clarifying our approach to mapping local cultural assets took a year's worth of regular meetings by university researchers on the CAMRA project with cultural planners at Wollongong City Council. Both parties were driven by a desire to broaden consultations in light of future cultural planning needs – to incorporate diverse views and thus open up the conversation about what constitutes creativity in an industrial city setting. CAMRA researchers also pursued specialist projects on specific *forms* of vernacular creativity (custom car design, surfboard shapers) and *sites* of creativity (for example, the Oxford Tavern, the live music venue, host to Wollongong's fringe/alternative/punk subcultures until its untimely closure in 2010).

To sufficiently capture Wollongong's cultural assets a mixed-method approach was required. Specific projects associated with Honours and PhD thesis projects meant it was possible to dedicate time and energy to locating and exploring alternative creative sectors beyond the usual places, while a series of other activities would be pursued by the project as a whole, with the broader population. A pragmatic approach was taken to initially select specific creative activities and sites: custom car design was a focus because of the authors' prior knowledge and awareness of a creative scene in Wollongong surrounding car design, which had also recently been demonised by mainstream media in the area as 'hoon' culture. The Oxford Tavern was chosen because of the involvement of one of the authors as a musician there. Surfboard shaping was chosen because another of the authors is a keen surfer and knew of the region's high-quality custom surfboard workshops – but also knew that surfboard makers felt frustrated and somewhat 'out of the loop' of decision-making in the city about cultural and economic planning.

It became apparent that a much more ambitious public research exercise would be needed to broaden the net. This latter exercise became the hosting of a 'cultural mapping lounge' at Wollongong's largest annual civic festival, Viva La Gong, in November 2009. The 'cultural mapping lounge' consisted of a stall, manned by staff and students and CAMRA personnel from the University of Wollongong (UOW) and the University of Technology, Sydney (UTS). At the mapping lounge members of the general public – literally anyone – were invited to have their say on two basic questions: 'What is the coolest place in Wollongong?' and 'What is the most creative place in Wollongong?' These two questions, although simple, were the product of many hours of debate within project partnership meetings. They were chosen because they invited people in a reasonably accessible, 'pop culture' format to reflect on their city, on cultural life, and on creativity. They addressed the core questions of our research (as outlined previously) but in a non-academic format and using language that engaged rather than alienated participants. Accompanying these questions, members of the general public were also asked to draw on a paper map of Wollongong – explicitly identifying their 'cool' and 'creative' places with blue and pink highlighter pens (see http://vimeo.com/77756380 for a video explaining the process). Drawing on advances made elsewhere on a previous project (see Chris Brennan-Horley's chapter in this book), these maps were later collated and combined within geographic information systems (GIS) technology to produce analytical and statistical reports on where Wollongong residents located 'cool' and 'creative' places. Overall, 205 people participated in this exercise, producing 160 interviews and maps (some participated as couples or as whole families, completing one interview and drawing on a single map).

What transpired was that instead of an empirical exploration of specific cultural planning themes, a looser narrative approach emerged within which the aim was to simply ask people about their experiences and then let participants narrate a story of their lives and of the role played by creativity and local culture. This narrative approach enabled a form of personal dialogue with researchers not possible through semi-structured interviews.

Vernacular creativity: A brief sketch

Results from our cultural mapping lounge were instructive. Although most of the 160 map interviews were brief, there were 2,355 drawings of 'cool' and 'creative' places on the maps – an average of fourteen per map. Some fifty hours of interviews were recorded, equating to 107,000 words of transcribed narrative material from a single day's research activity. Participants were from diverse demographic backgrounds, including whole families, retirees, students, farmers, motorcycle bikie gang members, Buddhist monks (Wollongong happens to be a major centre of Buddhism, featuring Australia's largest temple), steelworkers and well-known figures in the regional Aboriginal community.

Some overall findings were reasonably predictable. Wollongong city centre and nearby North Wollongong (a trendy beachside, inner-city area with apartments, cafes and a strong student culture, connected to the nearby university) were the two most commonly identified locations for cultural assets. And within them established arts and cultural infrastructure were repeatedly identified as sites of vernacular creativity activity. At the same time, however, the interviews revealed a scattered and diverse suburban geography of cultural and creative activities. Although the city centre and nearby North Wollongong were the most commonly drawn places on the map, they made up only 18 per cent of all responses. The remaining 82 per cent of sites for cultural assets were outside the city centre. Among the top ten 'cool' or 'creative' places were older, established middle-class localities (Gwynneville), working-class industrial suburbs (Port Kembla, Fairy Meadow) and tiny beachside villages to Wollongong's extreme north (Wombarra, Coledale). These top ten suburbs accounted for 55 per cent of all responses. The remaining 45 per cent of cultural assets (over 1,000 identified cases in total) were scattered across 65 other suburbs in the region.

Beyond an obvious concentration in the city centre is another, substantial, and decidedly suburban geography of cultural assets, with an accordingly heterogeneous mix of activities and attachments. There were numerous examples of vernacular, amateur, unusual and everyday, unheralded creativity: buskers, choir groups, writers' clubs, community gardens, markets, fire-twirling, belly dancing, linedancing, bluegrass nights, the local hardware megastore (a parallel to our earlier research in Darwin, where it too showed up as a creative networking place, specifically its paint aisle, a well-frequented place among visual artists), full-moon parties, sculpture gardens, garage bands, scrapbooking, graffiti-art (especially unsanctioned graffiti), the Nan Tien Buddhist temple, bike tracks, art shops and even a doll collecting club. Cultural activities and the contours of people's everyday relations to place are networked across city spaces, from central arts precincts to public housing estates, into hinterlands and leafy suburbs, beaches and national parks.

Sites of informal, prosaic creativity were documented and described by participants in response to the 'creativity' question (beachcombing for refuse to be used in garden sculptures, for instance); but, curiously, in face-to-face interviews some participants only cited examples of vernacular creativity in answer to the 'cool' places question, where they talked more freely and confidently:

> The community garden at North Wollongong's pretty cool... actually it's creative. I guess it's something out of the ordinary, a creative idea. They do create things using interesting materials.

They don't have a lot of funding or anything. They have to be creative and use recycled stuff that they go and find or source for free…wood and whatever, for garden furniture. (Female, 29)

Others were cranky with the concept of creativity, for its implicit elitism:

Interviewer: We're asking people where they think the creative places are in Wollongong, where's Wollongong's creative place?

Respondent: What a dreadful question. How elitist are you? I worked in Cringila for years – and I'll tell you what, when it came to creating the home grog and the vegetable gardens, even though it was grown in soils full of lead, it was extremely creative, right? Wherever there's human endeavour there's creativity. (Female, 54)

While many forms of creativity in everyday experience were captured by our map interview exercise, so too were critical voices questioning the very utility of 'creativity' as an analytical category.

On the whole, participants were more likely to identify their own suburb as 'cool' than 'creative', except for those living in the 'creative' hotspots of Wollongong, North Wollongong, Thirroul and Austinmer – who voted for their own suburbs as creative. Creativity was for many an abstract activity, associated with established cultural infrastructure in the city centre, whereas 'cool' places were closer to home, and in many ways more closely fitted with a broader, more inclusive concept of what constitutes cultural assets. There was also evidence of specialisation in the city – some suburbs were iconic 'cool' places on a regional scale, more so than they were 'creative' places, and vice versa. North Wollongong – with a historic pub popular with young people, a scenic beach, student share-house scene, cafes and nightlife – was a regional-scale 'cool' place, drawing people from across the entire city.

An almost perverse contrast was that of Port Kembla, which was the focus of much discussion as a cultural asset – but in ways cut across by class and place. Port Kembla is adjacent to the city's main steelworks, which has fallen into disrepair since the 1980s, following cutbacks at the steel plant, migration of working-class communities to new estates, and decentralisation of retail to large undercover malls on the city's edge. Shops in Port Kembla's Edwardian-era main street were abandoned and the area harboured unregulated street sex work, and had a reputation for madness, addiction, homelessness and dirt. There have been numerous attempts at revitalisation through place-making, public art and community schemes. In our research, Port Kembla showed up regularly as 'cool' and 'creative', but with a very peculiar twist. No one who rated Port Kembla as 'creative' lived there, and only two people (out of twenty) lived within adjacent suburbs. The remaining 90 per cent rating Port Kembla as creative lived to the (more affluent) north, especially from those suburbs – Wollongong, North Wollongong, Thirroul and Austinmer – that were rated the 'most creative' overall. No one from the working-class south side rated Port Kembla as 'creative' or 'cool'. Interview narratives provided an explanation: after attempts to reinvent it as a cultural hub, the idea of Port Kembla's creativity-led transition has permeated into some people's consciousness – but only, apparently, those who live in the more 'arty' parts of Wollongong. Creativity both amplifies and transgresses long-held geographical imaginations of the polarised city.

Making (and re-making) things: Surfboards and custom cars

In a city known for its manufacturing history, it should come as no surprise that discussions of cultural assets in Wollongong considered the physical making of things. We explored two sectors in detail, as sub-projects: surfboards and custom cars. The researchers already knew both of these anecdotally – but neither sector had been the focus of empirical research, nor considered as legitimate cultural assets in previous civic policy-making. The Illawarra region is home to a thriving surf culture, which is supplied by a smaller concentration of about a dozen local surfboard workshops, several of which have international reputations and export markets. Meanwhile, the region is a particular hotspot for custom-car enthusiasts, with a critical mass of automotive workshops, repair yards, mechanics and avid car users. How might these two examples of the material making (and re-making) of things come to be thought of as cultural assets in an industrial city setting?

Critical to understanding surfboard making as a vernacular cultural asset is the continued importance of craft-based forms of manufacturing, notwithstanding considerable challenges from automated production techniques and cheap, mass-produced imported surfboards. In Wollongong, as in other global surfing hubs, surfboards are still made by hand, by expert 'shapers' who plane and sand foam 'blanks', and 'glassers' who seal them against the elements. Because they are customised to local waves and body size, most Australian surfers ride boards made locally – even when cheaper imported boards are available. Surfboard making is a cultural asset in terms of the makers and their embodied skill: it is a tactile process, drawing on haptic skills by experts using their hands. Hand-based production is necessary to produce boards tailored to the surfer's individual body size, shape, preference, and local wave type. In interviews, shapers and glassers (who were universally men; women were employed in office and administrative positions) emphasised this system as craft, as art form, as well as production of a specialised sporting good. Such activities supported a local niche industry, but crucially, should be considered as a future *cultural* asset for Wollongong too.

Surfboard shapers learned their work informally, as low-paid helpers in workshops initially, then slowly graduating to more complex production tasks. Phil Byrne from Byrne Surf explains:

> We learnt from scratch, there's no formal training in shaping. I was able to go up and watch a shaper in Sydney who was making some

boards for me and he showed me what to do for a few hours and then it was trial and error. We started shaping in our grandparents' garage before I started working for John Skipp...after a while certain elements led us to starting our own business, around 1976... Everyone learns from scratch, no TAFE or formal stuff...It really is like that in most places – watch, listen and learn, all on the run.

In the surfboard making scene, craftsmanship, customisation and relationships between shapers and their customers are all sources of credibility and cultural capital. They are also important intangible assets for future cultural planning.

In custom car design, male and female participants from blue-collar backgrounds developed specialised knowledge about how particular custom parts (suspension systems, wheels, body skirting and engines) could be fabricated both to add unique visual appeal and to dramatically improve driving performance. At one level a set of practical skills with car parts, this was also revealed as an important set of cultural assets within working-class areas of Wollongong previously denigrated as 'uncultured' or 'bogan'. Car-customising knowledge was often only disseminated and accessed socially within a specific sociocultural scene. Thus what emerges is a form of design and production that is not just throwing parts together and attaching them to a car. Instead, work was a careful and richly creative process: ideas and designs were firstly hatched amongst social groups, informed by personal tastes and feelings; then, in performing custom car work, technical knowledge about mechanics, electrical wiring, restoration, painting, metal fabrication and upholstery became requisite – but only towards ends that emphasised idiosyncratic personal expressions and aesthetic preferences. Automotive industries may be archetypically blue-collar, yet they also enable rich forms of vernacular creativity: as talents, skills, knowledge and abilities are assembled to generate head-turning designs. This creativity was a quality developed through personal interests and refined by daily practices and social interactions working on them.

Whether aiming to produce a show car or customising as a hobby, local automotive workshops in Wollongong were central spaces. Business networks directly assisted fabrication of show cars, while enabling hobby car enthusiasts to source required parts, materials, and specialised knowledge. The businesses sought by participants to assist with production (and where participants were themselves employed) had very particular spatial tendencies, concentrated across Wollongong's light industrial estates. This shaped particular kinds of jobs and circuits for custom car production. A distinct regional geography of creativity was also revealed. If conventional categories of creative industries are mapped for Wollongong, work is concentrated in the inner city and wealthier northern suburbs. These are locations for the university, regional art gallery, performing arts and entertainment centres, and several music and visual art studios. By contrast, automotive employment and circuits of custom production were concentrated in older industrial estates close to the city's central business district, as well as low-density, suburban working-class, industrial areas to the city's south and west. These are the blue-collar neighbourhoods typecast as 'bogan', with high rates of youth unemployment, but which are central to the creative production of custom rides in Wollongong. Cultural assets were revealed in the seemingly most unlikely of places – car parts shops, paint shops, grimy and noisy automotive workshops – outside of the bourgeois creative city agenda.

A space for otherness: The Oxford Tavern

Our final example is of the Oxford Tavern, which for two decades was the central venue for Wollongong's alternative and punk music scenes. It was unambiguously a key cultural asset – even though it was frequently overlooked in the city's official creativity and innovation strategies. It illustrates the importance of documenting vernacular cultural histories of subcultural places within Australian cities and regions, taking seriously the forgotten venues where marginal social groups find meaning and community. Resonating are more universal themes in Australian cultural life: the formation of cultural scenes with dispositions towards accommodating, rather than resisting, difference; finding a space for otherness; and the importance of music and a physical performance venue in shaping a time and place of life transition from youth to adulthood.

Live music venues that are pubs often fall outside traditional policy structures and meanings of the arts, their fate determined less by formal cultural policy administration than by local regulations that diminish viability and by neighbouring urban processes of gentrification and noise pollution. Pubs as live music venues are frequently overlooked in creative city strategies, or, when present, construed as 'risks' to be managed.

One of the city's earliest pubs, The Oxford was originally built in 1845 as Elliot's Family Hotel. In the 1930s, its ornate Victorian frontage was replaced with an austere Art Deco exterior. The venue began hosting bands in 1989, and despite misguided revamps and lethargic management (at times bordering on neglect), it survived more than twenty years as the focal point for the city's underground, avant-garde, oppositional and left-of-centre music scenes. A participatory and communal philosophy present at the Oxford created a 'haven' for subcultures. This was not particularly the intention of the venue management. Indeed, throughout most of its history as a live venue, pub management reticently accommodated the music scene. Rather, a music scene colonised the available space, and in so doing, engendered a sense of belonging and community.

The Oxford stood in stark contrast to the city's other pubs and clubs, caricatured by members of the alternative and punk music scenes as crass 'beer barns', dominated by a monopolist company, the RDL Group, who owned/operated over half the city centre's licensed drinking venues. Musical diversity was part of the ethos of the Oxford Tavern – and upheld by key gatekeepers at the venue, fostering intense localism within the scene. In 2010, when we conducted our research, the Oxford advertised no fewer than eight musical genres: rock, acoustic, blues, metal, punk, groove, hip-hop and world. In interviews for this project, ninety-six different descriptors were used for those who went to the Oxford and what music was played there. Its true significance to supporting vernacular cultural diversity in Wollongong was perennially underestimated.

Exactly how this significance was achieved was by proactive and intensely pro-local decision-making on the part of the venue's booking agents. These agents acted on subcultural knowledge to include and exclude bands based on their allegiances to the 'scene'. Even more prominent in recollections was the extent to which band bookers also enabled forms of local creativity. They did so by establishing principles upon which decisions were made to book bands (or not), creating 'rules' that skewed booking practices in favour of local and original live music. Their ethos was to develop a musical performance space for emerging local bands unable to perform elsewhere. Bands were rewarded for their attachment to the Oxford, and for the sense of community and solidarity their continued attendance at the venue fostered.

Although associated most strongly with punk and alternative rock, the Oxford was home to a diverse range of subcultures and musical genres, enabling marginal groups to connect by collectively demonstrating their 'otherness' to mainstream Wollongong. In a small city setting, a single alternative venue accommodated sub-cultural difference and exchange, a force of necessity in a culturally conservative place with limited scope for venue specialisation.

Sadly, the Oxford Tavern closed its doors in 2010, during the conduct of this research, as part of a planned (and subsequently indefinitely delayed) urban redevelopment scheme that included the demolition of the historic hotel to build an apartment/shopping complex. At the time of writing the building still stands, empty and unused, in an increasingly dilapidated state. Although the Oxford was much loved and is fondly remembered by members of the local music scene, its demise remains a reminder of the gulf that still exists between the whim of real estate developers and aspirations to incorporate vernacular cultural assets into mainstream planning.

Conclusions

Looking back on research experiences, it becomes clearer why vernacular creative activities such as surfboard making, custom car design and punk music have until now been absent within formal civic cultural planning processes. In the past, certain creative cultures and endeavours (especially museums, theatre, visual arts) have had full-time employed managers who served as crucial gatekeepers interacting with civic gatekeepers of cultural policy and planning. What passes as legitimate within the sphere of cultural planning has been informed by societal perceptions of what counts as 'arts', or what counts as 'creative' – but is also a product of the professional networks within which policy discourses circulate. Other forms of vernacular creativity might be equally 'artful' but have remained invisible. This project sought to begin the process of breaking out of that cycle. Vernacular diversity and a small number of select forms of cultural assets were documented and are now on the radar.

Nevertheless, other forms of creativity were downplayed by participating community members: people doing custom car design, for instance, rarely perceived what they did as creative or artistic and were dismissive of council initiatives at inclusive cultural planning practice as being 'irrelevant' for them and their pastime. Customising cars was an outlet for personal expression, an avenue for doing something that was interesting outside the confines of boring, repetitive and tiring work in a blue-collar industry. Custom car designers could pull together different people and skills – friends they had in the local area – in ways that perfectly match academic descriptions of the network sociality present in creative industries. And yet they didn't see custom car design as particularly creative, or as a legitimate form of art. Thus a form of self-exclusion accompanied actual exclusion from previous policy discussions of art and creativity.

In the case of the Oxford Tavern, the city ultimately failed to view the venue as necessary or valuable cultural infrastructure, even though the city had sought to embrace discourses of creative city regeneration. Views about cultural assets from within music scenes are tied up in history and cultural meaning; such assets cannot be 'invented' overnight but rather emerge and gain credibility slowly, as experience accumulates over the years. Attachments to place provide cultural infrastructure with critical meaning as cultural assets through repetitive use, resulting in familiarity with a venue and its participants.

Ultimately, to engage with working-class people and places requires a reshaping of thinking about ways to encourage or develop community arts and creativity. It requires some measure on the part of local government towards breaking outside the 'enclosures' that form over time around policymaking spheres, as well as questioning accepted wisdom and existing regulatory practices where appropriate: such as with live music or handling community resistance to the staging of car shows in public spaces; issues to do with insurance, risk management, local traffic plans and waste management – all the bureaucracy that surrounds urban planning, festivals and events. From our work it becomes clearer that cultural planning outside the predictable frames needs action on quotidian themes such as these, which rarely feature in creative city strategies.

Regeneration Redux:
Hobart and MONA

Justin O'Connor

Introduction: A chance encounter

June is the cruellest month in Hobart, at least for the tourist industry. The city is the closest Australia gets to those dark Scandinavian winter nights, when the sun is on its way down as you come out of work, and it's dark before you get home. Last year, towards mid-winter, a beam of white light shot up into the grim clouds coming in from the ocean. Ryoji Ikeda's *Spectra* could be seen from all over the city, evening strollers lifting their heads from the rainy pavements to gaze. Tethered to the grounds of the War Memorial on the edge of the city centre, *Spectra* represented a new level of collaboration between the Museum of Old and New Art – MONA – and Hobart City Council. On the Salamanca waterfront, bonfires were lit and huge slabs of meat hauled over fires on machines of medieval torture, nobody noticing the absence of the Health and Safety inspectors, their acquiescence a part of the invisible stitching of the event. On the solstice, a naked swim event was snatched back from the hands of the local police, who wanted to ban it on grounds of public indecency, by the state and city authorities, fully aware of the impact such a ban would have on the island's image. Dark MOFO, Hobart's new winter festival, was warming the hearts (if not the arses) of locals, tourists, taxi drivers, restaurateurs, tourist agencies, city aldermen and Jetstar accountants alike. In the unlikeliest of places, arts-led regeneration was now back on the agenda.

Dark MOFO is the hibernal sibling of MONA FOMA, the museum's summertime Festival of Music and Art and Tasmania's largest contemporary music festival. First run in the island state's capital in 2009, its eclectic mix was an early indication of the ambitions of the relatively unknown Moorilla Museum of Antiquities, which had closed its doors in 2006 for a refit. Four years and around $75 million later, the refit was the personal vision of local hero and gambling millionaire David Walsh. As Nonda Katsalidis' building was being sunk deep into the rock below the heritage-listed former home of modernist architect Roy Grounds, Walsh's encounter with modern and contemporary art accelerated. In 2011 a new kind of iconic building – apart, mysterious, dark and Delphic – surfaced on the River Derwent, twenty minutes by ferry from Hobart docks.

At first glance, 2007 appeared a bad time to start a regeneration project. After two decades, the bright global urban future that was to have been kickstarted by a heady combination of *starchitecture*, *startists* and the ready availability of coffee had juddered to a halt. The regenerative effect of catering to the consumption preferences of the creative class – once a truth universally acknowledged – had largely failed to materialise. In an article in *The Daily Beast* – 'Richard Florida Concedes the Limits of the Creative Class' (2013) – Joel Kotkin, among others, noted that most damning was the admission by its academic-entrepreneurial proponent Richard Florida that his central claims were essentially flawed. The creative city had become a hubristic ruin, belonging to that other world, before the global financial crisis.

Yet, almost by chance, the surprise arrival of a 'world class' contemporary art museum in Hobart put arts-led – not culture-led but *arts*-led – regeneration back on the agenda. The script reads like a classic: multi-million-dollar art gallery transforms a cultural backwater in Australia's most economically challenged state.

Brimming with an astounding private collection of antiquities and modernities, Walsh's MONA was a private folly, a personal obsession made public at his own expense, and he didn't care in the least if it caused outrage amongst the good folk of Hobart. Bilbao's Guggenheim, the international gold standard of art gallery–led urban regeneration, had grown out of lengthy debates around the strategic role of culture in a post-industrial city. Hobart or, more precisely, the small city of Glenorchy next to the state capital, and one of its poorest areas – got MONA only because Walsh happened to be born there. That it was an instant hit, locally, nationally and internationally, took almost everyone by surprise. Whilst aspirant global cities wooed the various art-world franchises – Guggenheim, Tate, Met and MOMA, Louvre, Prado – or launched yet another biennale, Hobart got a unique global brand and attendant festivals dropped into its lap. Was it gift from the gods, or a Trojan horse? Or both?

In this chapter I want to look at how Tasmania and Hobart have responded to MONA, as part of a broader reflection on how art and culture are being used within the wider framework of the 'creative city'. In particular, how the tensions between 'culture' and 'economics' have been elided by the notion of 'creativity as resource', leaving a disconnect between a gratuitous 'art' and its relentlessly instrumental usage in regeneration.

In the elections of March 2014 all three parties put out cultural and/or creative industries proposals. Oddly, both Liberals and Greens shared the same language: the creative industries were a major economic sector, they were set to grow faster than any other and they should be supported through a 'peak body' and various creative space development schemes. Only the Labor manifesto mentioned the word 'culture' separately to the creative industries.

Among all the talk of growth, incubators and jobs, MONA was mentioned only briefly. The Greens wanted to make a \$5 million bid for a southern Guggenheim, 'as sister museum to MONA'; Labor would develop a cultural precinct around the MONA ferry pier. Yet everybody knows that the reason for the 40 per cent rise in Qantas flights to the island, for the phenomenal rise in the number and quality of bars, restaurants, hotel rooms and for the proliferation of cultural events, lies with the 400,000 visits made annually to MONA.

Despite this, we should remember that Hobart, in its pre-MONA days, was by no means the cultural backwater the in-flight magazines liked to depict. It had enjoyed a strong arts scene from the 1970s, though this is currently holed up in the historic, underfunded Salamanca Arts Centre. It had a thriving music scene. It was hanging onto the cultural infrastructure of an older, regional Australia, as it fought and lost the battle over the ABC but won the Tasmanian Symphony Orchestra. But the arrival of a global event such as MONA, like having a piece of designer furniture dropped into your nice comfy lounge, shook a lot of things up.

And, of course, David Walsh and MONA were strange beasts. Not the usual arts organisation – painstakingly preparing their hundred-page funding applications for twenty grand, knowing they'll get knocked back to ten – MONA's running budget of \$8 million a year puts the state's own arts budget to shame. How do you deal with such a thing? It was not just the money. The kind of cultural capital amassed under the cliffs of the Berriedale peninsula, the kind of people floating in from Melbourne and Sydney – *and beyond!* – all this somehow left the city for dead.

And yet it was immediately popular. This was not just about 'visitor numbers' – which they had in spades – but people *enthused* about it. They told their friends. They went on Facebook and Twitter. Groups of Young People were spotted. So too were older men in grey jogging pants – a demographic long since dropped from marketing's 'to do' list. MONA was a talking point. It was a must-see. And very soon the numbers began to make an impact. Restaurants were packed; new ones popping up all the time. Hotels were full. Taxi drivers got used to airport–Glenorchy fares. Money was coming in, disposable income was up. So what was the city going to do about it?

From cultural to creative cities

Visiting Hobart for the first time in late 2011, hearing stories and rumours about MONA, it reminded me of Manchester in the early 1990s. There, the city council had just stepped back from a Liverpool-style resistance to the Thatcher government's assault on 'socialist' local authorities. In the late 1980s Manchester had embraced culture-led urban regeneration as its way out of a rapid de-industrialisation that had challenged it not just economically but existentially. What was this city for? What could it be? Following the emergent regeneration script, it had parcelled up its heritage waterfronts – canals, not river or seafront unfortunately – and its nineteenth-century infrastructure as development opportunities. It was bidding for the Olympic Games (and remember, Barcelona's 1992 reinvention of their regeneration opportunities had not yet happened), building a concert hall and doing up its old art gallery. What the city council did not notice was that, whilst it was bussing a group of reluctant International Olympic Committee members around to sites on which they were implored to imagine shiny new stadia, the world's media was already in the city chasing young ravers through numerous dilapidated nightclubs and up and down its semi-derelict streets.

It took a few years for the penny to drop that the culture the city sought was as much on the streets – or in the clubs and garages and bedsits – as it was in the official festivals and buildings. It took a few years more for councillors and the local urban growth coalition to learn how to handle a globally famous music sector. They learned about culture and design, about using the right language, about herding cats and about dealing with big(ish) beasts who took a lot of drugs. The music sector – or at least the managers and the nightclub owners – learned about real estate development. In the process, the real and imaginary landscape of the city changed.

What this process entailed was a complex reinvention of the imaginary of Manchester. The unexpected arrival of a global music industry allowed the city to 'reimagine' itself. By 'city' I mean a complex articulation of music industry, local growth coalitions, the city council and the more popular discourses circulating in the local media. Manchester had become a 'city of culture' refracted through an organising imaginary in which its history as a 'shock city' of the industrial revolution – to use Asa Briggs' phrase from *Victorian Cities* (1963) – was reconstructed as future oriented. In the 'organising concept' developed by the city's creative director Peter Saville, long associated with Factory Records, Manchester became the *original modern* city.

It was a cultural imaginary that drew on those discourses of urban renaissance and 'culture-led regeneration' that dated back to the 1980s. In the United Kingdom this was strongly associated with the work of Charles Landry and Franco Bianchini but it could be found among the planning and architecture world represented by Peter Hall and Richard Rogers. The organising narrative was that of the Fordist city having (nearly) killed the city in its clunky top-down planning, over-regulation and exclusive focus on the industrial system of mass production, mass consumption and mass transit. The 'cultural' here meant not just arts infrastructure but also a retrieval of some older values of urbanity that had disappeared with the cleansing of the chaotic nineteenth-century city in pre-war and post-war planning. Deindustrialisation was an existential threat but it was also an opportunity for reinvention. Urban culture involved new forms of life in the city, where the production and consumption of culture represented new sources of identity, of employment and of a wider symbolic re-positioning of the city in the national and international arena.

Perhaps in Manchester, and in certain other places, such as Glasgow, this reinvention had some traction with the problems faced by cities experiencing deindustrialisation and economic challenge. However, from the late 1990s, as culture-led regeneration accelerated, a more uniform urban landscape began to emerge. In *A Guide to the New Ruins of Great Britain* (2010), Owen Hatherley mordantly charted this new urban terrain in which a 'post-Rave growth coalition' (a term he stole from me) led an 'urban renaissance', a return to the city centre in the form of cafes, art galleries, trendy apartments, boutique hotels, heritage shopping, restaurants, pubs and nightclubs. Many others have catalogued the kinds of 'urban imaginary' this art and culture-led regeneration has created. However, this urban imaginary goes beyond a consumption-led, CBD-centric process of gentrification. What we can see is a process whereby the cultural city meets the entrepreneurial city, making it ripe for a new descriptor and a new kind of guru: the 'creative city' and its theorist Richard Florida.

In the 'creative city', vibrancy in the form of street life, shopping and festivals is not an indicator of a recovery of older forms of urbanity. Instead, it becomes homologous with – indeed, is directly contributory to – the city's wider capacity for innovation and growth as a whole. Creativity is detached from 'culture' – which is now only one of its incarnations – and becomes a generalised resource across the whole city. However, art and culture do remain as privileged symbols of this wider creativity. If factory chimneys were a synecdoche for the industrial economy, art gallery cafes performed the same for the creative economy.

Creative was the keyword of the naughties. In the nineties it had been culture. Culture stood opposed to economics. That utilitarian, price-driven, tone-deaf discipline – the language of governments and bank managers the world over – was now getting it completely wrong. People followed their desires, not their wallets; they dreamed rather than planned; they wanted fulfilment not bovine security. Which meant, paradoxically, that culture was big business after all. All those once told to get a proper job were now proved right. There was more to life than economics; but this *more* was also to be a new source of economic growth. Was this a case of having your cake and eating it too?

John Holden, in *Capturing Cultural Value* (2004), explored this question in terms of the opposing intrinsic/extrinsic, but this did not quite capture it. There was 'economic impact' (and indeed 'social impact') and then some 'intrinsic value'. But what might this 'intrinsic value' be when very often the more that something had 'intrinsic cultural value', the more economically valuable it became. In urban regeneration terms, if it was not a quality cultural offer, then it was not going to add value to the local city. The word 'culture' retained this tension within itself. It was now a new economic driver but somehow it was different to, though generative of, economic value. 'Intrinsic' described not so much what this value was in itself; rather it marked out an empty or contestable space in which judgements of value were not reducible to economic impact.

'Creativity' removes this tension, though tension remains in the creative industries, which, no matter how hard we try, still refuse to gel into an entity that people can get a hold on. It provides the ground on which commensurability between the culture and economics can take place. Artistic and cultural creativity, for so long set against the drab rational-choice of neoclassical economics, is now a key resource. Creativity is about the production of the new; about solving old problems with different eyes. It combines the radical iconoclastic and generative energies of art with the innovation imperatives of the new cognitive economy. At the same time, the drive to self-creation associated with the artistic persona becomes generalised to everybody as an essential human capital resource. Creativity is not in any tension with economy; in the new Schumpeterian version of cognitive capitalism, the shock of the new functions across all domains of knowledge.

Creativity mobilises and de-differentiates all three aspects of Raymond Williams' famous threefold definition of culture in *Keywords: A Vocabulary of Culture and Society* (1976) — as a general human capacity, as a whole way of life and as privileged kinds of intellectual activity, especially art. In *The Creative Economy* (2001), John Howkins writes that it all becomes 'ideas' coupled to various intellectual property regimes. Florida's 'creative class' designates those who deal in ideas, which effectively means artists, creative industries and senior scientific, professional and managerial occupations. For theorists of the creative city, the long history of urbanisation and its characteristic features of inventiveness, economic intensity, sociocultural diversity and complex inter-connectedness were to be pressed into the service of the new creative economy. Initially a retrieval of a human scale and sense of urbanity from beneath the rusted planning mechanisms of the Fordist city, the creative city became a new imperative. As Sako Musterd and Wim Ostendorf write in 'Creative Cultural Knowledge Cities' (2004):

> Cities, which want to be innovative, to flourish and to offer wealth and employment to [their] inhabitants, feel that they have to adapt to arenas in which knowledge and creativity can develop. Culture is often added to this arena, not just as a condition to attract the creative knowledge workers, but also as a major economic sector, intricately interwoven with other sectors of the economy.

The creative city and regeneration

If we can characterise culture-led urban regeneration as a narrative in which the retrieval of an older urbanity is used as a basis for a new kind of city future, we also need to note that, from the beginning, it was linked to a specific set of claims from the arts and cultural sector itself. While I would reject the reduction of culture-led regeneration, and indeed the cultural industries agenda, to a tactical response to the decline in arts funding, it is nevertheless true that the two themes have run together. It is the 'having your cake and eating it' approach: arts and culture are valuable in themselves *and* they are at the cutting edge of the economic future.

We might say the first attempt to 'economise' the arts came not from Margaret Thatcher but from John Myerscough, whose report, *The Economic Importance of the Arts in Britain,* was published in 1988. He applied the 'multiplier effect' to the arts to show that for every £1 spent on an arts institution, £X were generated in the local economy. A version of this method was used by the Salamanca Arts Centre in 2013 to justify its demands for more state funding. Symbolic and 'reputational' aspects were less amenable to statistics, but case studies were rapidly accumulated by a growing number of cultural consultancies. This policy found its most dynamic expression in Bilbao's Guggenheim museum, inaugurated in 1997. It is the iconic gallery's iconic gallery. It stimulated an explosion of new arts building projects globally, most notably in China, where, from around 2006, Shanghai and Beijing began to vie with each other to become the cultural capital of China. At the same time, 'culture-as-lifestyle' also became part of the creative city mix.

Richard Florida's innovation was first, to extend the 'high' cultural offer from the photogenic institutions and events to 'lifestyle' cultures; and second, to provide statistical proxies by which these could be captured and ranked competitively. In the article 'Reconceptualising the Relationship Between the Creative Economy and the Recession' (2013), Andy Pratt and Thomas Hutton write that, for Florida, it was:

> the relationship, between niche cultural consumption and lifestyle, which attracts a particular segment of the labour force (the creative class) to cities, and in turn, as this group is in demand by emergent high-tech companies, they will 'chase' the workers and locate in 'creative cities'.

In their critique of both these tendencies – arts-led regeneration and cultural tourism, and lifestyle amenities to attract the 'creative class' – Pratt and Hutton suggest that they focus on cultural consumption at the expense of production. By stressing the economic dimension of the cultural/creative industries, the authors suggest that consumption-led creative city policies have failed to adequately address the specific needs of this sector in terms of an industry policy. They term a production-focused industry policy 'intrinsic', because it looks to the creative industries' specific needs not just their 'instrumental' use for tourism, inward investment and so on. However, they argue these are not like 'just any industry' but are ones with specific requirements and characteristics that have profound implications for policy.

An industry strategy would have to give full attention to the complex cultural dynamics at play here, the tension between cultural and economic value that has always been acknowledged by the cultural – but not the creative – industries tradition. It would need to deal with the ecosystem: the range of large and small businesses; the spectrum of commercial, state-funded, not-for-profit and voluntary agencies and actors; the institutional infrastructure; and the complex embeddedness in local place. The focus would not be on individual firms but on networks and projects, which would encourage a new approach to governance as a relationship between policy and sector that would build trust, knowledge and dynamic interaction, not just top-down policy silos.

This is a cultural ecosystem approach to the cultural/creative industries and is highly suggestive of future lines of policy development. But there are two main problems.

First, creative industry policies, as with creative city policies, have been rolled out under an 'economic imaginary' in which it is precisely the 'economic' benefits that are foregrounded. The need to understand and flexibly support the ecosystem in which the cultural industries operate has proved to be beyond policymakers. Creative industry agencies in the United Kingdom and Australia – between which there is a high degree of interaction – have been under-resourced, without any real power, separated from the wider arts and cultural policy, and are focused on 'commercial wins' of a highly restricted and short-term nature. As noted previously, the three main political parties in the 2014 Tasmanian state election rolled out creative industry policies that were different from other industry statements only in the paucity of real ideas. If we want economic deliverables, they seem to shout, then we need to use the language of economics.

However, the exclusive use of the language of economics to deliver cultural benefits ultimately undermines the value of culture. We have seen this in urban regeneration schemes, whether led by big arts and culture buildings or the more dispersed and informal promotion of creative clusters, incubators and so on. It is real estate that recoups the benefits and there is very little cities can – or at least are inclined to – do about this. More generally, however, despite Pratt and Hutton's brave attempt to use the needs of the cultural industries as a foundation for a progressive, responsive urban cultural policy, I think this cannot work unless two things also happen.

First, policy needs to break with the language of economics as it stands. This does not mean floating off into 'intrinsic value', leaving the dirty world of economics to its own devices. That would be disaster. Rather, a direct challenge to the dominant economic language is required, widening its scope to include the full range of formal and informal activities through which people make a living, and by which they exchange and acquire the necessary material and symbolic resources. The current language of economics can barely describe this, though it is not uncommon in the areas of sustainability, development and feminist and ecological geography. This struggle over what is 'economic' is at the heart of debates in Australia regarding manufacturing. It is not about whether this or that sector is viable – with the creative industries pushed forward as replacement – it is about what we mean by 'viable' in the short, medium and long term. Viable for whom?

Secondly, this effort needs to go beyond the language of economics and find a new language of value, one in which 'the economic' can find its 'proper' place. At the moment, apart from the *extremis* of national security and (possibly) health, there are no values that cannot be best secured by and through the economic imperative.

This is where I think the values of urbanity, of a more tangible, if sometimes fluid, mobile 'urban citizenship', of civic virtues and the good life — all those values that were part of that initial retrieval of the city in the 1970s and 1980s — can play their role. Cultural/creative industries and galleries like MONA provide a range of opportunities for making a living and for making a life that need to be acknowledged. These cannot be reduced to 'jobs and wealth creation' without excluding a whole range of benefits, and systematically misunderstanding how and why these cultural activities operate.

MONA

The chance encounter between MONA and Hobart, and with Tasmania, is not a 'policy problem', a disruptive splash around which the waters of a sensible cultural strategy document will eventually settle. The challenge and potential of MONA were quickly recognised by city and state, and it has energised many individuals in the policy umbra and penumbra. New levels of collaboration around the two festivals, as well as the year-round presence of MONA, have begun to make those active in the city think about what that city is and might be. The three election documents presented this in the standard script — Tasmania as creative industries hub, with incubation space and the requisite 'peak body' to draw up an industry strategy. But underneath this there has been a much more iterative and subtle engagement with the potential brought about by MONA.

A more relaxed attitude to planning and food safety regulations, the sensitive use of a war memorial site for an artwork, and, of course, the naked winter solstice swim — these are clear indicators of a new attitude. A deeper, more creative engagement is taking place as Hobart works with MONA to allow artists to 'rethink' particular city spaces and develop interventions. Again, it recalls the re-imagination of the urban landscape in Manchester (and not only there), whereby the junk space of a dilapidated nineteenth-century city was rediscovered by people looking at it differently – some with a view to development, but others as a reconnection with the physical and historical landscape in a new era.

These kinds of re-landscaping can be purely aesthetic, and that aesthetisation recouped primarily by real estate and its 'stunning' apartments, boutique hotels and fine dining. But they can also make us rethink what the city might be *for*. In *Dark Matter and Trojan Horses* (2013), Dan Hill uses the concept of the 'MacGuffin', Hitchcock's plot device – the secret plans, a necklace, a handbag – which is not particularly interesting in itself but just gets the characters and the plot moving. The design MacGuffin is the project that makes you think about the wider dynamics and vectors going on in the city. So Dark MOFO's Winter Feast sparked a range of applications for food vans, which in turn made many in Hobart city think about what food regulation was really about and how does food get into the city and in what form. MONA has been a powerful MacGuffin across a range of policy areas.

In its visitor numbers and its wide symbolic impact, MONA has certainly raised the profile of 'culture' in the city. The three creative industries strategies are testimony to this. The sad aspect of these is that the wider debate about what an economy is, what it can be, and the language by which it might be described and operationalised is being missed. The complex connections between food, art and tourism are just beginning to be debated, and they make for all sorts of interesting overlaps and intersections. Unfortunately, the election returned these debates to an older language of the 'culture wars'. Tony Abbott, as prospective Prime Minister, visited Tasmania and said it could never be a 'restaurant-led economy'. Subsequent state elections saw the debate turn to jobs, with economic growth and ecological conservation set against each other in zero-sum fashion. Both approaches instinctively found the zones of fear and resentment in Tasmania: the latte-drinking culture lovers, the tree huggers, lined up against the unemployed and the disenfranchised. Moments of fear and power politics are not (immediately) conducive to emergent new economic narratives.

It is the connection between the most abstruse, challenging, in-your-face art and its indisputable 'economic impact' that makes MONA interesting. How to respond to its arrival? Do you manage it, absorb it within (expanded) policy documents; 'leverage' its assets and impact for more arts funding; or demand more cultural clout in the planning committees; even launch a creative industries strategy? This will all inevitably happen. But what of other aspects? Art and music education in schools? New forms of cultural infrastructure and programming aimed at city and state populations? Perhaps a new approach to the planning and regulation of the city, not just a relaxation but a rethinking of what cities are and do. And a new vision of what culture can do for a city. Not as impact but as a space of curiosity, of challenge, of intellectual and emotional engagement, of the more-than-everyday, of meaning and self-transformation. A culture that is about how we live our individual and collective lives, and about how we might do this better and differently.

MONA then could be an opportunity to rethink what 'economy' is, but also to rethink what cultural policy is after three decades of its relentless reduction to economic impact and an equally damaging division into the (well-funded) arts and the terminally underfunded, social work of 'community arts'. MONA might mean the end of the creative city and the emergence of something new. Rather than an icon for the creative city, MONA may turn out to be its disruption or even détournement; what would a city look like *if it really was* creative? Undoubtedly, it will face the conservative challenge of the global art business, the local regeneration machine and a slew of new politicians whose main concern is business as usual.

Western Sydney: Developing and Implementing Cultural Policy

Penny Stannard

Across the breadth of Western Sydney today exists an impressive network of more than a dozen local government-run cultural venues. Each was a beneficiary of public funds provided through the Western Sydney Arts Strategy – a special cultural policy direction – that was in place from 1999 to 2011. The strategy was designed by the New South Wales (NSW) Government to stimulate cultural development in Western Sydney in order to rectify historical inequities that had existed in levels of arts funding in the region. The model was anchored on a $55 million local–state government cultural infrastructure investment program and an array of initiatives that sought to connect the region's diverse communities and its artists with these facilities to create new processes and material that would enable Western Sydney to author its place in Australia's contemporary cultural life.

Campbelltown Arts Centre is considered one of the great achievements of the Western Sydney Arts Strategy. Local officials refer to it as Campbelltown's 'jewel in the crown' and celebrate its recognition on Australia's cultural stage. Others, however, have equally observed that many residents do not even know that it exists and some believe that it is resourced to cater more for the needs of the inner-city Sydney cultural scene than the local arts community. These recent frictions are not unique to the strategy but illustrate the contradictions and ambiguities that emerge when cultural policy directions that are driven from the 'top down' intersect 'on the ground' with community cultural needs. There is a tendency to place these spheres in opposition to each other, as Katherine Knight's *Passion Purpose Meaning: Arts Activism in Western Sydney* (2013) implies. Yet, the situation is not so simplistic. The complexities that arise as these forces develop and meet can only be understood by detailed studies of particular places and Campbelltown itself provides a case in point.

This chapter engages with contemporary discussions concerning cultural policy directions in Western Sydney by investigating earlier precedents. It examines developments in cultural policy among three tiers of government – local, state and federal – and, in particular, how they converged in Campbelltown from the mid-1970s to 1981 to create a unique environment that would set the stage thereafter for an alliance between cultural policy directions and a local social movement that would ultimately result in the establishment of Campbelltown City Bicentennial Art Gallery (1988).

The approach towards this study has been through the field of cultural policy studies. It has also drawn on the disciplines of urban studies and public history. A literature review of government reports, policies and plans, media articles, scholarly material and recent interviews with people who have played a key role in community cultural activity and/or in the delivery of public policy in Campbelltown, have formed the research methodology. A series of questions was established at the outset to guide the critical analysis of research material: What were the forces that led to the meeting of cultural policy directions and community agendas in Campbelltown in the 1980s? Who were the stakeholders involved? How did Campbelltown's position within broader spatial and cultural landscapes impact upon the configuration of agendas? Why was the cultural agenda at the time channelled through the trajectory of a regional art gallery, and did this approach reflect the needs of the population in general? The consideration of these questions highlights how, beneath what might appear to be aligned imperatives, fundamental ambiguities continue to resonate within discussions about culture and the arts in Western Sydney today. Concluding observations provide readers with new knowledge to form fresh perspectives in how they interpret and understand the current cultural policy environment.

Cultural policy directions

The term 'cultural policy directions' is used here to encompass public support for cultural activity that extends from both ad hoc to formalised policy models. It places the arts as a focal point in examining cultural policy. While not suggesting that the arts alone constitute a definition of culture or are the sole concern of cultural policy, it follows the assertions of both Deborah Stevenson in 'Cultural Planning in Australia: Texts and Contexts' (2005) and Deborah Mills in 'The Necessity of Art' (2007), that cultural policy to a large extent becomes 'operationalised' through the arts and heritage spheres. David Throsby in *The Economics of Cultural Policy* (2010) locates the arts – music, literature, visual and performing arts – and creativity at the core of cultural policy as it is conceptualised through the cultural industries and represented through his concentric circles model. He maintains that rather than being understood simply as representing elite or 'high art' forms, these core categories offer a departure point for structurally positioning the gamut of multiple forms that fall within the domain of cultural policy. These understandings provide the theoretical basis for positioning cultural policy in relation to arts-based activity.

The Campbelltown City Bicentennial Art Gallery still exists today in the form of the exhibition spaces, workshop studios, residency apartment, sculpture garden, Japanese garden and cafe, which, when combined, make up a substantial proportion of Campbelltown Arts Centre.

Arts and culture in Western Sydney: Recent findings, recent debates

Few would doubt that the Western Sydney Arts Strategy has been successful in developing cultural infrastructure. Michael Volkerling, 'In Search of the Author of Contemporary Australian Life: Cultural Policy in Western Sydney' (2012), and Christina Ho, 'Western Sydney Is Hot! Community Arts and Changing Perceptions of the West' (2012), have each agreed that this is the case. However, Volkerling has suggested that the strategy's second core objective – to connect local communities with cultural infrastructure – has largely failed. Ho, on the other hand, has credited the strategy with having enabled such a flourishing of community cultural activity that it led to a 'cultural renaissance' and a re-imaging of Western Sydney's identity. The agency charged with this responsibility, Arts NSW, has acknowledged that the strategy contained some inherent and complex challenges within its brief to guide arts and cultural development across the entire Western Sydney region. Its reach across fourteen local government areas constituted a huge spatial conglomeration of diverse communities with vastly different needs. By incentivising partnerships with local councils, the strategy attempted to carve out a cultural policy approach that could be tailored to suit the particular needs of local areas. Regional coordination in the delivery of the strategy was designed to recognise local peculiarities while guiding them into line with the cohesive and systematic approach that the model offered.

Arts NSW's *Western Sydney Region Arts and Culture Snapshot* (2013) points to many contradictions and implies that a number of the strategy's core objectives remain a work in progress. For instance, the region is home to 'talented and resourceful artists' and there is a growing demand for local stories to be told. Yet local cultural resources are funnelled primarily into infrastructure, rather than towards the artistic development that is required to enable these homegrown stories to be produced by the region's artists. It would seem that councils successfully build local arts centres but are less effective in supporting local artists to develop through these facilities. This issue came to a head in a debate that sparked a furore in 2010 in Campbelltown, an area located in the southern zone of Western Sydney.

Claims were made in a local newspaper that the core cultural policy direction of Campbelltown City Council – its award-winning Campbelltown Arts Centre – was operating primarily to cater for the palate of 'the Sydney arts scene' – promoting up-to-the-minute Sydney-based sophisticate artists – while neglecting the needs of the local arts community. Defenders of the Arts Centre pointed to its recent success in gaining the competitively sought after 'multi-art form status' from the Australia Council, the federal arts funding body that is concerned principally with artistic development at a national level. This achievement signalled that the Arts Centre was recognised as part of the national cultural scene. While defending the Arts Centre in this vein, the Campbelltown Mayor also declared, paradoxically, that it should be 'the creative hub for the local arts community'.

Living in the '70s: Cultural policy agendas emerge

Back in 1973, Sydney's west and Australia's outer suburban areas featured in the inaugural cultural policy directions that the new Australia Council was developing to meet its obligatory functions. Places like Campbelltown were high priorities within the Whitlam Labor Government's program of renewal and reform, and cultural policy – 'the arts' – as it was then understood – came to be seen as an important and integrated component within this. In the Australia

Council's *Annual Report* that year, Chairman Dr H. C. Coombs observed that facilities to support the practice and enjoyment of arts were 'sadly lacking' in the less affluent, newer and growing suburban areas of Australia's metropolitan cities. The absence of this infrastructure, he stated, significantly compromised the Council's responsibility to 'widen access to, and the understanding and application of, the arts in the community generally'.

To rectify this, the Australia Council established a Community Arts Unit to identify which sections of the population were 'culturally disadvantaged'. Gay Hawkins observed in *From Nimbin to Mardi Gras: Constructing Community Arts* (1993) that the culturally disadvantaged were people who were united by a common bond of cultural deprivation caused by spatial, economic or social circumstances. Local government provided the Unit with a geographically coded space for defining 'community'. Recipients of welfare and social services also constituted 'community' in a non-physical sense. For Hawkins, this fluid definition of community enabled the Unit to encompass as many domains as possible in its remit, and constituencies for the community arts could be constructed around several axes simultaneously.

The Unit established a special initiative for Western Sydney and appointed field officers to 'liaise with groups and stimulate interest' in the arts. Rather than finding a 'cultural desert', as she had expected, Field Officer Helen Colman reported in 1976 that Campbelltown had a 'remarkably active cultural life at the local level' and offered a much greater range of cultural activities than other areas. Nevertheless, she recommended that a Community Arts Officer be appointed through the Australia Council's 50 per cent local government subsidy scheme to maintain and grow the local cultural sector further.

It wasn't until six years later that Campbelltown City Council established a position. During this time, the very existence of the Community Arts Program had been under threat. The new Fraser Government's widespread cost-cutting reforms had recommended that the Australia Council be made leaner and more focused on national cultural objectives. The Community Arts budget was to be slashed, but intense lobbying by funding recipients not only saw the program survive, but thrive. Its budget was increased to over $2 million, it was transformed into a fully-fledged board and the favourable evaluation of earlier initiatives validated its work. The Community Arts Board (later renamed the Community Cultural Development Board) now had much greater clout within the Australia Council, and, with more resources at its disposal, was in a position to re-enforce and accelerate its agenda to ameliorate cultural disadvantage.

Hawkins has maintained that from this environment grew a distinctive set of cultural practices and organisations that prescribed the community arts. The 'community arts practitioner' also emerged. These were arts workers who received grants, managed projects and ran arts centres, and by having these practitioners working 'in the community', cultural disadvantage could be mitigated more readily by those who experienced it.

While these developments had been taking place at the Australia Council, Campbelltown had become one of Australia's most recognisably disadvantaged areas. From the late 1960s Campbelltown had experienced unprecedented rates of development and had absorbed much of metropolitan Sydney's swelling population. Private developers and the NSW Housing Commission had created entire new suburbs on land that had been farmed since the mid-1800s. By 1981–82 more than 36 per cent of Campbelltown's population lived in public housing and within a few years, 46 per cent of the population would be aged under twenty. The effects of economic restructuring had hit Campbelltown particularly hard. The promise of employment in decentralised industry, which had lured many young families to Campbelltown in their quest for affordable suburban home ownership, had not eventuated. The high proportion of local people who were dependent on welfare payments led the Federal Member of Parliament, John Kerin, to describe Campbelltown in 1981 as 'a "welfare electorate" par excellence'. Campbelltown had also developed a bad image due to media reports that perpetuated a narrative of outer suburban despair and dysfunction. Taking all these factors together, Campbelltown offered a ripe environment for the intervention of the community arts via the Australia Council. Cultural policy directions being pursued by the NSW State Government at the time also intersected within this context.

Led by Premier Neville Wran, Labor had formed government in NSW in 1976. According to Graham Freudenberg in *Cause for Power: The Official History of the New South Wales Branch of the Australian Labor Party* (1991), NSW Labor continued implementing, albeit at a slower pace, much of the agenda that Whitlam had introduced at a federal level, which included funding for the arts.

Apart from fulfilling its responsibilities towards major cultural institutions, the state government's overarching cultural policy principle was to make the arts accessible to the broadest range of people possible. Wran believed that the arts had been the domain of society's 'elite', so his government would focus on the cultural needs of, among others, the working classes, migrants and those who lived in regional NSW. Western Sydney was a priority region.

The government's primary cultural policy objective was to improve the standards of housing for the arts. It introduced a capital assistance program to provide matching state funds to local government funds for infrastructure projects. This model was especially geared towards priority regions and additional support was provided to councils to employ professionally trained directors in regional galleries and museums. More people would have access to the arts if facilities existed in their hometowns, and communities would experience a greater number and higher quality of programs if appropriately qualified people managed these venues. The result would be a reduction in levels of cultural disadvantage in populations across NSW. Thus, while the state government was aligned rhetorically with the Australia Council in respect of the amelioration of cultural disadvantage, the mechanism with which it chose to deliver this policy objective was vastly different. And while it did provide some funding for the community arts, its path was largely set on building infrastructure to institutionalise the arts within communities.

The case of South West Sydney was unique, however. Here, the state government implemented a variety of cultural policy approaches via the formation of the South Western (Metropolitan) Regional Arts Development Committee (SWMRADC) in 1980. Jointly funded by the Community Arts Board and the NSW Division of Cultural Activities, the SWMRADC could support community arts activities, promote regional arts development and focus on cultural needs and professional cultural positions simultaneously. Its aim was to encourage councils to increase their support for the community arts, foster arts activity and access in communities and schools, and promote the importance of the arts in society across the local government areas of Bankstown, Camden, Campbelltown, Fairfield, Liverpool and Wollondilly. Chairperson of the SWMRADC was Mary Seaman, a Campbelltown alderman.

Campbelltown and the convergence of policy-driven forces

By 1981 a series of policy-driven forces converged both conceptually and on the ground at Campbelltown. The Community Arts Board had prepared a ten-year nationwide strategy to encourage and develop greater levels of participation by local government in the community arts, and aimed to further grow its arts officer subsidy scheme. The state government was supporting the promotion of the community arts regionally in South West Sydney with a Campbelltown alderman at the helm, and it was funding local councils to build cultural facilities in regional areas.

Campbelltown became the logical place to host a Community Arts and Local Government Seminar in June that year. The NSW Local Government Association, the Community Arts Board and the NSW Division of Cultural Activities sponsored the event, which was coordinated by the SWMRADC. The seminar addressed 'broad issues' around local government involvement in the community arts, including employment of community arts officers, provision of community arts centres and support for community arts activities. David Throsby presented, explaining that the community arts could be thought of as a public goods benefit that delivered economic returns to communities, while other speakers emphasised its social benefits.

A new cultural policy was adopted later that year at the NSW Local Government Conference. It acknowledged that local government had a 'significant responsibility' towards the provision and encouragement of increased opportunities for the appreciation and participation in the arts, and it recognised the rights of communities to access and determine their own forms of creative expression. The policy directed that councils provide a range of cultural resources, delegate planning and management functions to the community, and enter into joint undertakings for the provision of regional and specialised cultural facilities. It stressed that councils should enact their powers to employ arts personnel and provide funds for 'innovative and pilot programmes'. (Under the 1919 NSW Local Government Act councils could provide, control and manage art galleries and support other cultural endeavours.)

The significance of the Association's new policy was that the community arts and the philosophies and practices that they encompassed were endorsed as legitimate council activity. From this point, the community arts were less on the periphery within local government than had been the case previously – something that had been especially true in councils that were serving large, growing metropolitan areas, as Australia Council consultant Murray Edmonds observed at the time.

In October 1981, Campbelltown City Council held a 'Social Futures Seminar' – a forum for residents, community groups, government and voluntary agencies to voice, and offer solutions to, the issues facing residents. Participants were asked to imagine how Campbelltown would be by 1986.

The tone was set by MP John Kerin, who gave the opening address, and the prominent local solicitor John Marsden, who gave the response. Kerin was unapologetically political. He critiqued shifts that had occurred in the ideology and management of the nation's economy under the conservative Fraser government, the consequences of which, he maintained, had impacted negatively upon communities to the degree that, within Australia, there were now populations, including his electorate, which were segregated economically and socially from the mainstream. His view was that Campbelltown would not change by 1986 while the current regime continued. Marsden's response laid the blame for Campbelltown's ills firmly with governments – on all sides of politics – for the poor planning policies that had created entire welfare dependent suburbs that were cut off from central services and support, the result of which had been segregation within Campbelltown itself.

The seminar indicated that new attempts were being made within council to embark upon social planning. A social planner position had been introduced in 1975 and Michael Knight had been appointed to the role. Knight has recalled that rather than being able to establish social planning methodologies within council during his three-year tenure, the administrative reality and the needs of the community dictated that he take on a service-delivery role. With social planning back on the agenda in 1981, the community arts was included as part of the mix.

The seminar's community arts workshop participants decided that what was needed to guide the future was a 'Campbelltown and District Cultural Development Plan' – a 'local environment plan for the arts'. This would bring together individuals, government, non-government and commercial stakeholders to support the provision of adequate space for the exhibition of two- and three-dimensional objects; adequate facilities for live performance; community education facilities for post-school arts education; local community-use spaces for arts activities; and encourage 'a diverse cultural identity that draws from both the old and new elements of Australian society'. The plan's most important aim would be 'the determination to develop Campbelltown and [the] district in the cultural and artistic directions that its community wishes and is prepared to work for'.

Workshop participants had voiced what they thought were impediments to these goals. For example, they felt that there was an attitude within government that the provision of cultural resources were not considered to be an essential service or need, but to be utilised only by society's elite. They thought that politicians seemed to accept the 'myth' that 'the mass of Australians are ockers, interested only in sports, television and drinking'. They observed that there was no common voice that could lobby on all levels of government on behalf of the arts in and for Campbelltown.

Change and contested concepts of cultural disadvantage

Some interesting issues arise when examining this process and its findings. The yet-to-be-developed cultural plan already had a set of very specific outcomes – an art gallery – that would operate to generate a new cultural identity for Campbelltown that straddled its past and present. A sense of work ethic seems to have qualified the individuals who would assume the reigns for advancing this, which, when measured against both Kerin and Marsden's presentations, would have probably excluded many within the local population. The local cultural spokespeople appeared to be frustrated by the lack of attention they thought they received from those operating in the political realm, while at the same time, they seemed to have realised the extent of their limitations in this respect.

Workshop participants concluded that the findings made by Helen Colman in 1976 still held true but had intensified. Her recommendation for a community arts officer was re-endorsed and a job description was prepared based on her original findings. This time around there was confidence that the position would materialise, as aldermen and senior staff were reported to 'solidly support the creation of this job'.

Yet, in grounding the position in Colman's findings, there was a fundamental misalignment with the principles of the community arts that the Australia Council espoused. Colman's research methodology had involved interviewing people who were already participating in Campbelltown's flourishing local cultural life. Rather than researching the needs of people that were culturally disengaged, as the Community Arts Board had based its entire premise on, Colman had studied the needs and aspirations of Campbelltown's arts community itself. This had not been her intention at the outset, however. She had attempted to engage with people who were not participating in organised cultural activities, and she particularly sought to find out more about the needs of young people. Outside of the school environment, cultural activities for them were non-existent. When she had broached this with the research interviewees, their responses had been invariably fraught with tension. While some had a vague sense that something should be done to provide cultural activities for Campbelltown's young people, many others vehemently opposed any special allowances for them. Yet statistics and social changes indicated that young people were forming an increasingly significant proportion of the population and would require specialised initiatives to meet their needs. Despite her efforts, the voices and needs of young people were very limited within Colman's work. It was those already actively involved in Campbelltown's local artistic life who were determining how it should further evolve.

For this 'community', cultural disadvantage was understood by Campbelltown's geographic separation from Sydney. While established cultural institutions and arts organisations were based in central Sydney, the entire Western Sydney region was, in comparison, grossly under-resourced. Such a geographic perspective alone would not take into account that cultural disadvantage also existed in relation to social and economic conditions, and those who were cumulatively disadvantaged on these fronts were the thousands of young families, migrants and others who had settled in Campbelltown through the affordable and public housing schemes that drove the city's suburbanisation. They embodied a modern Campbelltown and they were cut off from its established community activities, networks and services, which included those that made up Campbelltown's cultural life.

Representatives from organisations such as the Campbelltown Art Society, the Festival of Fisher's Ghost Committee and the Campbelltown Theatre Group, which had all been established between the mid-1950s and mid-1960s, had promoted their needs and future aspirations to Colman. These groups had sustained a local cultural life in Campbelltown over the decades. Indeed, as former Member for Campbelltown Graham West has suggested, their very success stemmed from how they had celebrated Campbelltown's sense of separateness to Sydney. But by the early 1980s, some of the voices leading these organisations embodied what Suzanne Jones has suggested was an 'old Campbelltown' – symbolic of a time, a place and a community that had existed prior to the onslaught of urban growth and development in the 1970s. These changes, Michael Knight has observed, were so substantial and so rapid that, for some, 'Campbelltown changed under their feet'.

Between 1976 and 1981 the impact of growth and sub-urbanisation had been clearly felt within Campbelltown and had influenced its sense of identity enormously. But while it had changed significantly during this time, the voices of an older Campbelltown resonated at the forefront of its future cultural development. The challenge for the incoming community arts officer would be to act on the needs and advance the ambitions of the local arts community while, at the same time, deliver the Australia Council's objectives of ameliorating cultural disadvantage by inscribing the community arts – its ideology and its practices – within Campbelltown. In the first instance, this would involve the very specific goal of developing a regional art gallery, to rectify geographic-based cultural disadvantage. The second case would require working with people in the community whose needs encompassed more than one axis of disadvantage and who, to date, had not been part of Campbelltown's cultural development. Added to this were newly created expectations in local government of what the community arts promised as a means to build community and create local identity. On top of these complexities were the shifts that were underway in the political landscape as Campbelltown and its civic leaders were coming to terms with what it meant to be a modern, outer suburban city with its much-loved country-town image facing symbolic obliteration at the hands of a rising narrative of despair and community dysfunction. These forces combined would have constructed a highly complex environment and the situation facing the inaugural community arts officer would have been unique. It would take a special person to succeed in this role – someone who would have the skills and experience, both creatively and politically, to understand and cultivate these competing and contradictory forces and be able to deliver what was required by cultural policy imperatives that were driven from the top down and those that the community itself desired. So while recent discussions concerning Western Sydney and Campbelltown have provided an insight into the tensions that occur between cultural policy directions and local community cultural need, an examination of the situation two generations ago indicates that the contradictions and ambiguities that we see today are by no means a recent phenomenon.

Of Art, Ants and Capital:
An Aboriginal Artist in
Far Western New South Wales

Eddy Harris

I am Eddy Harris from Wilcannia, part of the Bakandji tribe, and I am a local artist from this area. I was born in Wilcannia, lived here most of my life; went away when I was about fourteen, went away to school for one year but came home again and started working, yeah. My family's from here. My mum is a Bakandji woman and my dad is a Ngurrampaa man, from Hillston in New South Wales. So I got a cross-section of tribes but I go under Bakandji, which means river people.

We had an exhibition in 2009 in Broken Hill [at the Regional Art Gallery], me and my four brothers. That was special to us... Broken Hill Regional Art Gallery accepted a letter from us, we wanted to do an exhibition and the gallery gave us a couple of dates and it was September what we picked so that was a really big event. We brought a cross-section of people through the gallery and the gallery people highlighted it later on in conversation, that amount of people that came and showed respect and gave us good feedback. That was a really good thing. I'd like to see a fair go with all artists in Wilcannia, and so I know I could put a bit of effort into bringing artists forward. In talking to them the right way with respect, talking to people the right way and coming down to peoples' real level.

We had a good exhibition in 2010 in Sydney [at Brush Farm House]…My brother Waddy Harris, nephew Alfred Harris, and other community artists and myself [exhibited at Brush Farm], and so we had a fair few pieces there. We had ceramics and wood, prints, canvas paintings, so we had a full range of art and artefacts coming out of Wilcannia. We got a lot of feedback from that and the quality of gear, the quality of the art and the feeling, and I think that's a really important thing for high-profile people to feel that because it's not a muck-around art. People were amazed… what the quality was like…That's not putting tags on us but I think that we deserved that respect because well me, I find we don't stop here. We just keep going, we just keep painting, we just keep carving because that's what we do. We…do other jobs as well, but in our spare time that's what we are about and that's our way of getting our message across I guess to the outside world.

This is us, this is us as people and we got to be recognised soon for what we do. In saying that I would just use top-end artists – for example, no disrespect to those people, they done amazing things, but we amazing people as well down this area even though our skin's lighter and eventually people got to understand that we are connected to the land as well, as Aboriginal people even though we fair coloured. We don't tell everyone our story…because no-one's asked, but through the artwork they're starting to feel that.

I do my art early in the morning, afternoons, and sometimes at night. See now, a lot of daylight saving so I can knock off work…it is an issue…a big issue. Especially when you work so hard and you haven't got a name out there and you got to respect our Dreaming out this way and I guess that's what I was talking about when I talked about the top-end people. I want people to see Aboriginal art. We don't exist and somehow us Aboriginal artists in New South Wales we got to change that. And I'm not blaming anyone. I think we've been patient long enough. I mean we'll eventually put Wilcannia on the map in this area. We don't just do it for Wilcannia. We do it for the area.

For example, in 1991, I was finishing on the mines. I used to work on the mines in Broken Hill as a supervisor, sharpening drill bits for the miners round the clock. I had two guys working under me and worked for an American company and the mines were closing down so I had to look for another avenue, so I started painting sandshoes. I painted little lizards and snakes, turtles and fish, yeah, on sandshoes and the locals in Broken Hill started buying them off me when I finished at the mine, so there we go. I said: 'Oh yeah, that's right, I remember my old uncles carving boomerangs on the riverbank out of river red gum and my brother used to carve them in the bush out of mulga wood and bring them in and show us, the yellow and dark brown colours coming through beautiful…that's what I'll do'. My brother is one of my elders and he is still carving boomerangs and is well connected to the land. So me and a couple of my brothers and some cousins started an art shop in Broken Hill selling artefacts, paintings and the sandshoes and we were getting 50 per cent of what we sold and the rest went back into the shop to keep it functional. It was a way of teaching the people here, local people, and then moving aside and giving them opportunities to teach themselves. They keep that going for the children and all that there.

I always wanted to do art, but in the old days the old people wanted you to get education. But artefacts and making things were always around and you always see it but you don't ask too much about it. You got to watch. Only if they call you over then they'll tell you something. But I remember my childhood really good, so I got a clear mind on how I think and that's why I got a lot of visions on how I can paint and what I can paint.

I don't just paint a picture; I paint a story. I paint a story. That's what I feel and seen out there and I've been told bits and pieces of stories by the old people, and as you go along and go to the bush collecting artefacts…I see different things and feel different things and then it all comes together and then I just paint. In saying that, you can go a little bit too far too because you've got to balance it all up…because you're doing all different jobs and if you don't balance it up, well then…

I've just got to be flexible in what I'm doing I guess…and plan it out myself. I've got a range of skills. For example, I have worked with National Parks as a tour guide, and I sit on the Joint Management Advisory Committee for Paroo-Darling National Park. I do a little bit of mentoring for young people; they come and talk to me every now and then. I'm an art teacher as well. I've got Certificate IV in Aboriginal Arts and Cultural Practice from TAFE. People come to me with opportunities – I see them as a challenge, to see where we can go with it.

In my artwork I tell a story but it all depends how many people are going to listen and if I can get it out there. That's why getting a profile, a proper profile, is important. It's not just important to me. It's important to give stories so the stories can be recognised that, yes, these people are connected to the land. They still have their stuff. That's why I do it.

I guess up in the top end of Australia and all that they got the curators that go into communities and look at the artwork and talk to the artists and say: 'Well, would you like an exhibition? We'll promote you and we'll get you the buyers and the paperwork, copyright, all that there'. And that's what they do. That's the kind of thing we need out here. You need a curator to come out here and likewise the other way round as well – the person on the ground needs to go and see the gallery and how it will look and see that everything is in order to get a good outcome. Just keep an eye on the art: I know how many days a person put into a painting and I can talk to the curators, who might say it's worth only $200 or something. We need to teach the next person these skills to help our people. We do this so [there's] a better life for ourselves and family…we'll put the money in here, in a savings account, for if your child wants to go to college. You're allowed money to support that. I want a crack at the top. I aim high and if you work hard enough, you deserve that.

I paint from the heart. It's not bullshit stuff. This is serious to me and my brothers and our connections to our land. We don't carve and paint for nothing and if people want it that's fine, if they don't want it, we just keep it. But it would be good to get seen a little bit more than what we have been.

I carve wood and all that and I said to myself well, I've got to start painting now. I done a lot of paintings earlier but I [had to]... find something that's special...so going to the river there with my brother to collect timber for our artefacts, and just walking around and seeing some of the sites where our people lived, and then I seen these ants and one was dead and the others were carrying it. We was having lunch and I chucked a bit of bread and they carried that and they came together again and they kept coming together and I said, 'Gee yeah that's it, ants. They're like us. Yeah, they come together when someone pass on and they come together for a meal like we do and most of the time these here ants carry over their weight like us'. So I started painting ants using background colours to represent daylight or sunsets and sunrise. I am using the ants and they're one of my trademarks for my artwork...there'll be different colours and there'll be different stories to them...it's been really popular at my exhibition and getting a lot of comments on this stuff so hopefully, yeah, just keep going. For example, [in] *Daylight Gathering* the yellow in the painting represents the sun, and there is some white in the centre that represents the ash from the camp fire, and the ants represent the people; the big ants are the old people, and the little ants are the young people and they're teaching them about different stories and sites.

I started ceramics at the school. They've got a program for parents and their children, to come to school in the afternoon and do some designs on the ceramics, and they run classes on the weekend as well for the children. That's been very popular so what I do, I go along as well, I do some designs in black and white and a bit of brown and I call them the *Kangaroo Dreaming,* and they're a bit different than the ants. So I've got all these different styles, so now and again I do a landscape as well, but ceramics

Figure 1. *Daylight Gathering* (Image courtesy of the artist).

is really exciting once they fired and it looks good. But I do the stories to them too, so that's important.

I've had a few events. I've done a big public work up at Beechworth, up in Victoria there. On the lake, that was a really big project with the shire up there 'cause they couldn't get an Aboriginal person to come up with a concept, and I heard about it through TAFE in Albury so I went up there. Had a yarn to the project officer. Went away and drew a concept up, what I was going to put down on the ground. It was a walkway. Victoria Health gave me money, the arts didn't give it, but Victoria Health said: 'Yeah, this is a great program because it's a walking trail'. So they had the Chinese, Scottish, Ned Kelly themes and then they wanted Aboriginal. So I made a couple of big pieces in stone and rock and work with the local tribe to come and put some language in and, yeah, that was a pretty big project. It's there now and got a big information board up and everything and, yeah, that was a big thing.

A few friends from Dubbo area talked about Art Unlimited, which is a $3,000 art prize for best hanging art, donated by the Pro Hart family from Broken Hill. So I decided to enter it in 2011 with a big ant painting, 1 × 1 m, which they hung too low and it should have been hung high so that you can look into it. I'm not having a go or anything, but I took that as a lesson, so I went back to the drawing board and I've seen the art space now, so I said, well, I think I will have another crack at this and see where I can go with this with my other designs. Each year they have different judges from different towns and galleries. So in 2012 I entered *Kangaroo Dreaming* which was black and white lines, and then in 2013 I won this prize for the second year running with my *Claypan Spirit*. In 2012 I was also the finalist in the $40,000 Parliament of New South Wales Aboriginal Art Prize. It's a big thing, a reality check I guess, going in a competition. It is a big step; it could go either way, from filling out the application and sending it in, and actually getting the painting done and what feedback you get – whether you are prepared to take the good with the bad. Being a finalist and a winner, people then start to look for your work. You get publicity.

A couple of years ago I attended a gallery 'speed-dating' workshop held in Orange. Top Sydney galleries came along and I was one of the artists; there was just two Aboriginal people out of a group of roughly fifteen artists. It was a good opportunity to have my five minutes with top curators and galleries. I had a bit of a portfolio, not too much – to the point – what I'm about, where I'm from, plus a couple of pieces of my artwork. They get a quick look at it and ask you a few questions; this is a big reality check. I felt a bit sorry for some of the other artists who didn't get the feedback they were hoping for. So I went there from Wilcannia with an open mind, I know what I'm about and what I do. It went good. Some galleries don't deal in Aboriginal art but they tell you upfront; they deal in oils and landscape. I take their comments very seriously. I listen. But I got interest from one of the top galleries in Sydney. There is an opportunity there, but I think looking at percentages and all that, it didn't suit me. They are now good friends. Maybe one day we will look at an exhibition.

I've got a lot of stuff that I've got to do and paint and get out this message I guess, and I've got to get it out there to help our people to go forward. So if they see me comin' and goin' other people might break a circle and they might come and go, yeah, like myself and my brothers…That's why you get frustrated sometimes with that because you're carrying a lot of weight especially when you talk about the cultural stuff…It is an important thing and we're carrying it and we're not going to get an easy ride and everyone hits brick walls and stuff. But it's just a little bit harder when you're an Aboriginal artist trying to break ground. We've also got to be careful on what we paint and how we paint it because we always get this: 'Oh they're not dot paintings as in Western Australia and not really Aboriginal'. You've got to take all that as well. That's part of the art game, but the art game to us is our life. It's not just art. It's kinship and the more we get that across, some of us [will] break through the barriers for our people I think. Better. It'd be better for communities as well…You're connected with the land. You know where you've got to go to get your materials and all stuff like that if you want to make up clap sticks or if you want to make a dish, so you know the area, you know your timber and you can resource it.

Getting some of the other resources can be a problem. You've got to travel away to get your art gear. Your paints and wax and all that, canvas, you got to travel 200 kms to Broken Hill to get it. Then there's getting framing and sending gear away. I sent a painting and carving to Sydney…they just chucked heavy stuff on it and smashed the stick and it went through the painting, so I had to re-do another painting. Freight is a real problem.

We need a management team that connects all these people and works closely with us. We need someone to do the bookwork; I can't be an artist and a manager. I already tried that; it don't work. I done BEC [Business Enterprise Centre] training in Broken Hill for three months, so I know what it's all about. Things would be easier if I had someone here dedicated to what I'm doing so I go to them and I say: 'Right, I need to get in contact with this person and that person in this gallery, can you email that off now or nice letter and blah, blah, blah', and then organise when I'll be in Sydney on such and such, accommodation, meet with that person, flights or bus or whatever. We need that kind of thing here because we're isolated.

I've been on the Internet for ages but it's not been much of an advantage. Not at this stage, but I've been doing a little bit of stuff on the Internet. I'm just getting used to it and getting used to computers because I need to go forward. I can look up artists and what's happening in the arts and stuff like that, there you see who's who. I see a lot of upcoming artists. Because I want to be a professional artist, I have to be a professional manager, but I can't do both.

What we've got to start is getting money for individuals. Co-ops been given grants for years. Even though we're connected as family, we've still got our own minds and we like to be business men and women individually. I think that's where we need to look instead of giving money to co-ops all the time; we need to give it to artists who really want to go forward, put their energy into something. Monitor it if you have to, that's fine. But really put something into that person if they really want to go somewhere. I think we're lacking in that area. In the long run, it's for your community. If we talk about Wilcannia, the future is tourism. We can be similar to Broken Hill because it's so rich in history here. We've not only got Aboriginal history of 2,000 years, this is Bakandji traditional area; we've also got the history of the first Europeans, the river; this was one of the biggest inland ports for the steamboats to take the wool up and down to the towns, and beautiful old sandstone buildings from the local quarry. But we need money to start business, some incentives. Here, maybe the council can give you a building or say, 'Here, have this for twelve months and pay rent after that'. I was part of developing Broken Hill's Aboriginal art and cultural offerings, so I know what I'm on about.

SELECT BIBLIOGRAPHY

Lisa Andersen and Margaret Malone (eds), *All Culture Is Local: Good Practice in Regional Cultural Mapping and Planning from Local Government*, University of Technology Sydney ePress, Sydney, 2013. Available free online.

Alison Bain, *Creative Margins: Cultural Production in Canadian Suburbs*, University of Toronto Press, 2013.

Jeremy Beckett (ed.), *Wherever I Go: Myles Lalor's 'Oral History'*, Melbourne University Press, 2000.

Chris Brennan-Horley, 'Multiple Work Sites and City-wide Networks: A Topological Approach to Understanding Creative Work', *Australian Geographer*, vol. 41, 2010, pp. 39–56.

—— and Chris Gibson, 'Where Is Creativity in the City? Integrating Qualitative and GIS Methods', *Environment and Planning A*, vol. 41, 2009, pp. 2295–614.

Asa Briggs, *Victorian Cities*, Odhams Press, London, 1963.

Jean Burgess, 'Hearing Ordinary Voices: Cultural Studies, Vernacular Creativity and Digital Storytelling', *Continuum: Journal of Media & Cultural Studies*, vol. 20, 2006, pp. 201–214.

Manuel Castells, *The Rise of the Network Society, The Information Age: Economy, Society and Culture*, vol. 1, Blackwell, Oxford, 1998.

Michel de Certeau, *The Practice of Everyday Life*, Steven Rendall (trans.), University of California Press, Berkeley, 1984.

Jacques Derrida, *Archive Fever: A Freudian Impression*, Eric Prenowitz (trans.), University of Chicago Press, 1995.

Directorate-General for Internal Policies, *The Culture Strand of the Creative Europe Programme 2014–2020*, prepared by Colin Mercer, Nina Obuljen, Jaka Primorac and Aleksandra Uzelac, Policy Department B: Structural and Cohesion Policies, Brussels, 2012.

Peter Dunbar-Hall and Chris Gibson, *Deadly Sounds, Deadly Places: Contemporary Aboriginal Music in Australia*, UNSW Press, Sydney, 2004.

Graeme Evans, *Cultural Planning: An Urban Renaissance?*, Routledge, London, 2001.

Richard Florida, *The Rise of the Creative Class: And How It's Transforming Work, Leisure, Community and Everyday Life*, Pluto Press, North Melbourne, 2003.

—— *Cities and the Creative Class*, Routledge, New York, 2005.

Ben Gallan, 'Gatekeeping Night Spaces: The Role of Booking Agents in Creating "Local" Live Music Venues and Scenes', *Australian Geographer*, vol. 43, 2012, pp. 35–50.

—— and Chris Gibson, 'Mild-mannered Bistro by Day, Eclectic Freakland at Night: Memories of an Australian Music Venue', *Journal of Australian Studies*, vol. 37, 2013, pp. 174–93.

Chris Gibson, 'Creative Geographies: Tales from the "Margins"', *Australian Geographer*, vol. 41, 2010, pp. 1–10.

—— '"Welcome to Bogan-ville": Reframing Class and Place Through Humour', *Journal of Australian Studies*, vol. 37, 2013, pp. 62–75.

——, Chris Brennan-Horley, Beth Laurenson, Naomi Riggs, Andrew Warren, Ben Gallan and Heidi Brown, 'Cool Places, Creative Places? Community Perceptions of Cultural Vitality in the Suburbs', *International Journal of Cultural Studies*, vol. 15, 2012, pp. 287–302.

——, Ben Gallan and Andrew Warren, 'Engaging Creative Communities in an Industrial City Setting: A Question of Enclosure', *Gateways: International Journal of Community Research and Engagement*, vol. 5, 2012, pp. 1–15.

Ross Gibson, *Seven Versions of an Australian Badland*, University of Queensland Press, St Lucia, Qld, 2002.

David Grogan and Colin Mercer, *The Cultural Planning Handbook: An Essential Australian Guide*, Allen & Unwin, Sydney, 1995.

Owen Hatherley, *A Guide to the New Ruins of Great Britain*, Verso, London, 2010.

Jon Hawkes, *The Fourth Pillar of Sustainability: Culture's Essential Role in Public Planning*, Cultural Development Network (Vic.) in association with Common Ground Publishing, Melbourne, 2001.

Gay Hawkins, *From Nimbin to Mardi Gras: Constructing Community Arts*, Allen & Unwin, Sydney, 1993.

Dan Hill, *Dark Matter and Trojan Horses: A Strategic Design Vocabulary*, Strelka Press, St Petersburg, 2012. Available at: http://www.strelka.com/press_en/dark-matter-and-trojan-horses-dan-hill/?lang=en

Christina Ho, 'Western Sydney is Hot! Community Arts and Changing Perceptions of the West', *Gateways: International Journal of Community Research and Engagement*, vol. 5, 2012, pp. 35–55.

John Holden, *Capturing Cultural Value: How Culture Has Become a Tool of Government Policy*, Demos, London, 2004.

John Howkins, *The Creative Economy: How People Make Money from Ideas*, Allen Lane, London, 2001.

Charles Landry, *The Creative City: A Toolkit for Urban Innovators*, Comedia/Earthscan, Near Stroud, UK, 2000.

Marcia Langton, 'Well, I Heard It on the Radio and I Saw It on the Television', an essay for the Australian Film Commission, Sydney, 1993.

Tess Lea, Susan Luckman, Chris Gibson, Donal Fitzpatrick, Chris Brennan-Horley, Julie Willoughby-Smith and Karen Hughes, *Creative Tropical City: Mapping Darwin's Creative Industries*, School for Social and Policy Research, Charles Darwin University, Darwin, 2009.

Carol Liston, *Campbelltown: The Bicentennial History*, Allen & Unwin, Sydney, 1988.

Susan Luckman, *Locating Cultural Work: The Politics and Poetics of Rural, Regional and Remote Creativity*, Palgrave Macmillan, London, 2012.

Kevin Lynch, *The Image of the City*, MIT Press, Cambridge, MA, 1960.

Colin Mercer, 'From Data to Wisdom: Building the Knowledge Base for Cultural Policy', 28 September 2003. Available at http://ssrn.com/abstract=2153369 or http://dx.doi.org/10.2139/ssrn.2153369.

Deborah Mills, 'The Necessity of Art', *Dialogue*, vol. 26, 2007, pp. 33–42.

Tony Mitchell, 'Blackfellas Rapping, Breaking and Writing: A Short History of Aboriginal Hip-hop', *Aboriginal History*, vol. 30, 2006, pp. 124–37.

George Morgan and Andrew Warren, 'Aboriginal Youth, Hip-hop and the Politics of Identification', *Ethnic and Racial Studies*, vol. 34, 2011, pp. 925–47.

Sako Musterd and Wim Ostendorf, 'Creative Cultural Knowledge Cities: Perspectives and Planning Strategies', *Built Environment*, vol. 30, 2004, pp. 189–93.

John Myerscough, *The Economic Importance of the Arts in Britain*, a report for the Policy Studies Institute, London, 1988.

New South Wales Ministry for the Arts and the New South Wales Government's Office of Western Sydney, *A Strategy for the Arts in Western Sydney*, Sydney, 1999.

Jon Newman, 'Harry Jacobs: The Studio Photographer and the Visual Archive', in Paul Ashton and Hilda Kean (eds), *Public History and Heritage Today: People and Their Pasts*, Palgrave Macmillan, Basingstoke, UK, 2012, pp. 260–278.

Justin O'Connor, 'The Cultural and Creative Industries', in Greg Young and Deborah Stevenson (eds), *The Ashgate Research Companion to Planning and Culture,* Ashgate, Aldershot, UK, 2013, pp. 171–83.

Val Plumwood, 'Shadow Places and the Politics of Dwelling', *Australian Humanities Review*, vol. 44, March 2008. Available at http://www.australian humanitiesreview.org/archive/Issue-March-2008/plumwood.html.

Andy Pratt and Thomas Hutton, 'Reconceptualising the Relationship Between the Creative Economy and the Recession: Learning from the Financial Crisis', *Cities,* vol. 33, 2013, pp. 86–95.

Margaret Roberts (ed.), *Collected Verse of John Shaw Neilson*, UWAP, Crawley, WA, 2012.

Leonie Sandercock, *Cosmopolis II: Mongrel Cities in the 21st Century,* Continuum, London, 2003.

George Stavrias, 'Droppin' Conscious Beats and Flows: Aboriginal Hip-hop and Youth Identity', *Australian Aboriginal Studies*, vol. 2, 2005, pp. 44–54.

Deborah Stevenson, *Cities and Urban Cultures,* Open University Press, Maidenhead, UK, 2003.

—— '"Civic Gold" Rush: Cultural Planning and the Politics of the Third Way', *The International Journal of Cultural Policy*, vol. 10, 2004, pp. 119–31.

—— 'Cultural Planning in Australia: Texts and Contexts', *Journal of Arts Management, Law & Society*, vol. 35, 2005, pp. 36–48.

—— *Cities of Culture: A Global Perspective,* Routledge, Abingdon, UK, 2014.

Randy Stoecker, *Research Methods for Community Change: A Project-based Approach*, 2nd edn, Sage, California, 2013.

David Throsby, *The Economics of Cultural Policy*, Cambridge University Press, Cambridge, UK, 2010.

United Nations, *Creative Economy Report 2013 Special Edition: Widening Local Development Pathways*, UNESCO and UNDP, Paris, 2013. Available at http://www.unesco.org/new/en/culture/themes/creativity/creative-economy-report-2013-special-edition/.

Michael Volkerling, 'In Search of the "Author of Contemporary Australian Life": Cultural Policy and Research in Western Sydney', *The Nordic Journal of Cultural Policy*, vol. 15, 2012, pp. 192–203.

Andrew Warren and Chris Gibson, 'Blue-collar Creativity: Reframing Custom-car Culture in the Imperilled Industrial City', *Environment and Planning A*, vol. 43, 2011, pp. 2705–22.

—— and Chris Gibson, *Surfing Places, Surfboard Makers: Craft, Creativity and Cultural Heritage in Hawai'i, California and Australia*, University of Hawai'i Press, Honolulu, 2014.

Cameron White, '"Rapper on a Rampage": Theorising the Political Significance of Aboriginal Australian Hip-hop and Reggae', *Transforming Cultures e-Journal*, vol. 4, 2009. Available at http://epress.lib.uts.edu.au/journals/index.php/TfC/article/view/1070

Raymond Williams, *The Long Revolution,* Penguin, London, 1965.

—— *Keywords: A Vocabulary of Culture and Society*, Croom Helm, London, 1976.

Phil Wood and Charles Landry, *The Intercultural City: Planning for Diversity Advantage*, Earthscan, London, 2008.

Greg Young, 'Behind the Venetians', *Australian Planner*, vol. 37, 2000, pp. 14–19.

—— *Reshaping Planning with Culture*, Ashgate, Aldershot, UK, 2008.

——, Ian Clark and Johanna Sutherland, *Mapping Culture – A Guide for Cultural and Economic Development in Communities,* Commonwealth Department of Communications and the Arts, Canberra, 1995.

—— and Deborah Stevenson (eds), *The Ashgate Research Companion to Planning and Culture,* Ashgate, Aldershot, UK, 2013.

AUTHOR BIOGRAPHIES

Lisa Andersen works in industry policy and research with the Creative Industries Innovation Centre and, from 2009 to 2013, she was senior researcher on the Australian Research Council–funded CAMRA Project: Cultural Asset Mapping in Regional Australia. Cultural sector roles have included manager of the Empty Spaces Project; manager of audience and market development with Regional Arts NSW, and marketing manager of the inaugural Paralympic Arts Festival as part of her work for the Sydney 2000 Olympic Arts Festivals. Lisa is a PhD candidate at the University of Technology, Sydney (UTS), a member of UTS Research Centre for Creative Practice and Cultural Economy, and, for seventeen years, was community engagement coordinator with UTS Shopfront Community Program where she supervised 285 pro bono student-community projects in the areas of business planning, design, communications and research. Her publications include the books *All Culture Is Local: Good Practice in Regional Cultural Mapping and Planning from Local Government* (UTS ePress, 2013, co-edited with Margaret Malone) and *Making Meaning, Making Money: Directions for Arts and Cultural Industries in The Creative Age* (Cambridge Scholars Press, 2008, co-edited with Kate Oakley).

Professor **Paul Ashton** is head of Public History at University of Technology, Sydney's Faculty of Arts and Social Sciences and co-director of the Research Centre for Creative Practice and Cultural Economy. Paul was one of the founders of the Shopfront, UTS, where he has been director since 2004, and he has been involved in community engagement since his appointment at UTS in the mid-1990s. Paul has acted as judge for the NSW Premier's History Awards and Literary Awards. He has also been involved in numerous history-based community projects including the Northern Beaches Councils' (ShoroC) oral history project on the 1930s and with the Italian Cultural Association CoAsIt's project Sydney's Italian Fruit Shops. Paul's work on

'Australians and the Past' – which looks at how people use history in their daily lives – and with post-1960 civil memorials has received Australian Research Council funding. A board member and editor of the Dictionary of Sydney and an editor of the journal, *Public History Review*, Paul's publications include *People and Their Pasts: Public History Today*, co-authored with Hilda Kean (2008), and with Professor Paula Hamilton (UTS) he co-authored *History at the Crossroads* (2010).

Sue Boaden is a leading Australian cultural strategist based in Sydney and works around the country. Her projects are diverse and have been commissioned by clients in large metropolitan and urban cities as well as in regional towns and rural and remote areas. Her clients are mainly drawn from the public and community sectors including federal, state and local government, as well from as a range of arts and cultural organisations. Sue has nearly twenty years' experience in strategic cultural planning and policy development, in operational management reviews, in cultural and arts facility planning and management and in public library planning and management. Sue has an emerging interest in cultural impact assessment. She maintains an active focus in working with communities to build local identity and sense of place and has experience in public art policymaking and commissioning, as well as in making digital oral histories and storytelling.

Dr **Chris Brennan-Horley** is currently a DECRA research fellow at the University of Wollongong. His research interests include using GIS for cultural research, including integrating GIS techniques with qualitative methods; applying historical GIS to understanding rural cultures; and exploring patterns of work in the cultural and creative industries. His PhD (completed in 2010) combined mental maps and GIS to bridge between qualitative interview data and quantitative measures of the creative city. Outputs generated from this research challenged existing theories of where creativity resides in the city. Dr Brennan-Horley is currently the recipient of an ARC Discovery Early Career Researcher Award: 'Experiments in Space: Geospatial Information Technologies for Cultural Environmental Research' 2013–2016. By harnessing the power of emerging digital mapping technologies, this research will extend how we understand the relationship between humans and their environment. Specifically it will use maps to generate new knowledge across two important yet everyday problems: bushfire management and urban quality of life.

Rob Evitt is a PhD candidate at the University of Wollongong. His degree is a Bachelor of Science with a major in Human Geography. He is currently researching Indigenous hip-hop under the supervision of Professor Chris Gibson and Dr Andrew Warren.

Ben Gallan is a PhD candidate at the Australian Centre for Cultural Environmental Research (AUSCCER) at the University of Wollongong. His research project – 'Crepuscular Geographies: Rethinking Day and Night in the City' – seeks to critique the normalisation of day and night in literature and debates concerning night-time economy, parenting, urban exploration, and light pollution. Previous and ongoing research interests also lie in cultural infrastructure, heterotopia, music venues and scenes, night-time economy, parenting and urban theory.

Professor **Chris Gibson** began at the University of Wollongong in 2005, after holding lecturing positions at University of New South Wales, the University of Sydney and the University of Western Sydney. He is currently deputy director of the Australian Centre for Cultural Environmental Research and ARC Future Fellow. Professor Gibson is a member of the Australian Council of Learned Academies Expert Working Group, 'Securing Australia's Future – Australia's Comparative Advantage', and international expert contributor to the *2013 UN Creative Economy Report*. Professor Gibson ran the Cultural Geography Study Group of the Institute of Australian Geographers for several years, as well as a node of the ARC Cultural Research Network (2005–2009). He was also Discipline Chair for Human Geography in the Excellence for Research in Australia (ERA) 2010 assessment exercise. His most recent book is *Music Festivals and Regional Development* (2012, with John Connell). With Andrew Warren, he is co-author of the forthcoming book *Surfing Places, Surfboard Makers: Craft, Creativity and Cultural Heritage in Hawai'i, California and Australia* (University of Hawai'i Press).

Professor **Ross Gibson** is Centenary Professor in Creative and Cultural Research at the University of Canberra. Recent works include *The Summer Exercises* (2009) and *26 Views of the Starburst World* (2012), both published by UWAP.

Eddy Harris is a Bakandji man, born and raised in Wilcannia on the banks of the Darling River in far western New South Wales. Eddy works in three different mediums – painting on canvas, ceramic design and carved wooden artefacts. A recognised Bakandji Elder, Eddy has been teaching art and cultural practice through TAFE and various other organisations for much of his adult life. He is passionate about using his art to tell the stories of his people and to promote an appreciation for his culture.

Dr **Miranda Johnson** is an historian of indigenous peoples and settler colonialism in the Anglophone postcolonial world, most specifically in North America and the Pacific. Her work engages questions of race, culture and rights in legal, political and social contexts. She is currently completing a book manuscript, *The Land Is Our History: Law and Indigeneity in Settler States, 1967–2000*, which examines the production of a notion of indigeneity in sites of law as indigenous peoples struggled for their rights in the era of decolonisation. At the University of Sydney, Miranda holds an appointment as a postdoctoral research fellow in the School of Philosophical and Historical Inquiry, Faculty of Arts and Social Sciences, and in the Centre for Values, Ethics and the Law in Medicine, Faculty of Medicine, as part of Professor Warwick Anderson's ARC Laureate Fellowship project, 'Race and Ethnicity in the Global South'.

Margaret Malone is the managing editor of *Gateways: International Journal of Community Research and Engagement*, and was the co-editor of *All Culture is Local: Good Practice in Regional Cultural Mapping and Planning from Local Government.* She has more than twenty years' experience in publishing non-fiction books and journals and currently divides her time between participating in large-scale collaborative projects, such as the CAMRA project, and mentoring emerging academics and students in the development of peer review–ready research articles.

Professor **Justin O'Connor**'s career has included appointments at various universities in the United Kingdom, China, and Australia, and he is currently Professor of Communications and Cultural Economy at Monash University. During his time at Manchester Metropolitan University, Professor O'Connor led a Masters in European Urban Cultures, jointly offered by universities in Brussels, Tilburg, Manchester and Helsinki. His research led to the establishment of Manchester's Creative Industries Development Service (CIDS), the UK's first dedicated local economic development agency for the creative industries, of which he was chair. His interest in the developing international agenda for the creative industries has seen him speak in China, Malaysia, South Korea and Taiwan. Justin is currently leading an ARC linkage project, *Creative Clusters, Soft Infrastructure and New Media: Developing Capacity in China and Australia,* partnered with Shanghai Jiaotong University, the 'Creative 100' cluster (Qingdao) and Arup (Sydney). This is a systematic investigation into the evolving uses of creative clusters in China and Australia, with special reference to the role of social media and urban informatics in urban creative ecosystems. He is also a partner on a new ARC linkage project looking at the social, cultural and economic effects of MONA on Hobart, Tasmania. He has published over 100 books, papers, chapters and reports in the field of cultural and creative industries, arts and cultural policy, urban cultures and popular music. He is currently finishing a book for Sage, *After Creative Industries*; is working on a joint book on *Cultural Economy in the New Shanghai* (Routledge); and co-editing *The Routledge Companion to the Cultural Industries*. He is one of twenty international experts appointed under the UNESCO/EU Technical Assistance Programme in support of the 2005 Convention on the Protection and Promotion of the Diversity of Cultural Expressions.

Dr **Emily Potter** has a background in literary and cultural studies, with a particular interest in literatures of the environment, postcolonial literatures, and environmental cultural studies. She has published widely in these broad fields, with a particular focus on questions of place and place-making, belonging, environmental and critical theory, and political ecology. Current research projects include a three-year ARC Linkage project (with Janet McGaw, Anoma Pieris and Graham Brawn) on the politics of constructing Indigenous cultural centres in Australia (a book of this project, *Assembling the Centre*, will be published by Routledge in 2014); and a monograph, 'Fieldnotes on Belonging: The Politics of Place in Contemporary Australia' (to be published by Intellect in 2014).

Penny Stannard is a PhD candidate at the University of Technology, Sydney. Her research examines the tensions, ambiguities and contradictions that arise when suburban Australia is placed within the cultural policy discussion. Of particular interest are the intersections that occur between the physical and imagined dimensions of suburbia and how these are encapsulated both theoretically and 'on the ground'. Penny has had a twenty-year career producing contemporary cultural programs for organisations across the government, community, education and not-for-profit sectors. Her work spans disciplines of practice and is informed by methodologies that engage communities, researchers, policymakers, educators and artists in partnerships that result in creating new cultural material and influencing policy directions.

Professor **Deborah Stevenson** is Professor of Sociology and Urban Cultural Research in the Institute for Culture and Society at the University of Western Sydney. Her research activities and interests are focused in particular on arts and cultural policy, cities and urban life, and place and identity. Her recent publications include *The City* (2013); *Cities of Culture: A Global Perspective* (2013) and *Tourist Cultures: Identity, Place and the Traveller* (2010). In addition, she is co-editor of the *Research Companion to Planning and Culture* (2013) and *Culture and the City: Creativity, Tourism, Leisure* (2012). Professor Stevenson is an editor of the *Journal of Sociology* and the *Journal of Policy Research in Tourism, Leisure and Events* and a member of the editorial boards of several journals, including the *International Journal of Cultural Policy*. Her research program has been supported by external funding from a range of sources, and she has been a chief investigator on six grants from the ARC with her most recent ARC Discovery projects being 'The City after Dark: The Governance and Lived Experience of Urban Night-Time Culture' and 'Culture Circuits: Exploring the International Networks and Institutions Shaping Contemporary Cultural Policy'. Professor Stevenson has worked as an advisor and consultant to all levels of government and is currently a ministerial appointment to the NSW Arts and Cultural Policy Reference Group.

Dr **Andrew Warren** is an economic geographer who completed a PhD as part of CAMRA in 2012. His thesis examined the surfboard industry and was focused on east-coast Australia, southern California and Hawai'i. Dr Warren now works at the University of New England, where his research is focused on three interconnected themes: regional development, socio-economic change and employment relations. As an economic geographer he engages with these themes by combining cultural and political economic theory with empirical research. Some of his previous and ongoing work focuses on such topics as the global surfboard manufacturing industry and its regional geography (a topic on which he has recently completed a book); the production, recording and commercial performance of music in rural and remote Australia; contesting the future of Australian manufacturing and industrial regions; and the precarious work experiences for those employed on a (sub)contracted basis.

A/Professor **Greg Young**, MPIA, is Adjunct Associate Professor, Urban and Regional Planning, Faculty of Architecture, Design and Planning at the University of Sydney. He has a significant international reputation as an innovative scholar and as the author of a number of landmark planning and cultural strategies developed as an executive and consultant to the Commonwealth, state and international governments. Greg was a contributor to Australia's first National Cultural Policy *Creative Nation,* and co-authored with AIATSIS the Australian model for cultural mapping, *Mapping Culture – A Guide for Cultural and Economic Development in Communities.* His publications include the influential *Reshaping Planning with Culture* (2008), which contains his concept of 'culturisation' and 'culturised planning' now utilised in research and teaching in Scandinavia and other parts of Europe. He is also principal editor of *The Ashgate Research Companion to Planning and Culture* (2013) and a Member of the International Review Panel, *Revista Crítica de Ciências Sociais*, Portugal. Earlier in his career Greg was the first historian appointed to the NSW Heritage Council where he was also a planner and the Council's advocate. A former chair of the Sydney Harbour National Park Advisory Committee, in 1997 he was awarded the inaugural NSW Premier's Max Kelly Scholarship to Venice, Italy, and in 2014 a Getty Fellowship at the Getty Conservation Institute, California, USA.

www.ingramcontent.com/pod-product-compliance
Lightning Source LLC
Chambersburg PA
CBHW040254290326
41929CB00051B/3378